THOUGHT POWER

By

SRI SWAMI SIVANANDA

Double 9 BOOKS

THOUGHT POWER

by **SRI SWAMI SIVANANDA**

ISBN: 978-93-59394-25-1

Published by

DOUBLE 9 BOOKS
2/13-B, Ansari Road, Daryaganj
New Delhi - 110002
info@double9books.com
www.double9books.com
Tel. 011-40042856

ABOUT THE AUTHOR

Sri Swami Sivananda, the famous author of "Thought Power," stands out as a lighthouse of knowledge and kindness in the spiritual sky. Swami Sivananda was born on September 8, 1887, in Pattamadai, Tamil Nadu, India. He began a life devoted to self-realization and making the world a better place. His journey took him through both faith and medicine, and he became a successful doctor at the end of it. But he gave up his medical business and became a renunciate because he wanted to learn more and help people in a deeper way. Even after his Mahasamadhi (spiritual freedom) on July 14, 1963, millions of people are still inspired by Sri Swami Sivananda's life and work. Because of his deep spiritual insights, kind heart, and unwavering commitment to helping people, he is a revered figure in the pantheon of spiritual luminaries and is seen as the personification of knowledge and love.

CONTENTS

Preface....7
Chapter 1. Thought Power—Its Physics And Its Philosophy....9
Chapter 2. Thought Power—Its Laws And Its Dynamics....18
Chapter 3. Value And Uses Of Thought Power....29
Chapter 4. The Functions Of Thought Power....35
Chapter 5. The Development Of Thought Power....40
Chapter 6. Thoughts—Their Varieties And Their Conquest....46
Chapter 7. Positive Methods For Thought-Control....54
Chapter 8. The Patterns Of Thought-Culture....63
Chapter 9. From Thoughts To Thought-Transcendence....73
Chapter 10. The Metaphysics Of Thought Power....78
Chapter 11. Thought Power For God-Realization....87
Chapter 12. Thought Power For A New Civilization....92

Preface

This instructive book carries in itself a life-transforming value. None who reads it, with the needed interest and attention, will ever feel inclined to remain unchanged in personal nature and untransformed in conduct and character. A good deal of careful judgment and confidence would assist us in asserting that no one who reads this work, will fail to resist the readiness to make of his own will a Power that alters and exalts his own life and destiny. The work is fraught with implicit guidance for turning our personalities into forces of compelling influence and charm, and for rendering our lives into so many grand stories of the epic unfoldment of the Divine Truth we enshrine, the Divine Light we bear, and the Divine perfection we hold in our inner being.

This, then, is a simple, straightforward, inspiring book that holds out many methods for the culture and nurture of thought power. It is also a work that presents us with many useful suggestions which enable us to reach a region beyond the terrain of thought and its power, a realm of transcendental Experience and God-consciousness.

Helped by his own illimitable Love for all humanity, and dictated by the logic of his untiring energies for the service of every man, Sivananda has made himself extremely useful to all kinds of people, to men in all walks of life, and has written books on a rich diversity of themes in his own illuminating and spiritual way. Embodying in himself the very spirit of the whole of Indian spiritual culture, Sivananda has poured out on mankind hundreds of gifts of the books that enshrine Wisdom of Life. The present work will commend itself, and will yield many rewards, to both the lay public and the community of spiritual individuals. It will be found very valuable more particularly by persons who, while not believing in any religion, not given over to love any God, not subscribing to any article of faith, are yet eager to live a life of power, purity, peace, prosperity, progress, happiness and fulfilment, right in the environs of their work-a-day world.

Sivananda has attempted implicitly to present in this work, a dynamic knowledge of thought power at these three distinct fields:—

1. *The field of higher applied psychology*: Here Sivananda speaks of thoughts ; forces that chisel countenance, fashion character, change destiny, and ıake of life an all-round success.

2. *The field of a full-fledged parapsychology*: This field is covered by ıose widely scattered passages and chapters in this work, which throw lumination on the fact that human Mind is the seat and centre of a number f supernormal powers and factors. Sivananda urges the readers to tap ıese powers, and to make operative in their own outer life, the various igher faculties they command.

3. *The field of transcendental realization*: Wherever Sivananda prescribes method for, or speaks of thought-transcendence, he is attempting to lead s into the domains of Divine Realization in which thought ceases to be ıought, and blazes into infinite Consciousness.

This work, then, represents Sivananda to the readers, in a way, ; a practical psychologist, a physicist and chemist in the world of the henomena of thought, a parapsychologist, a Yogi, and thus helps them uild their future, gain their success in life, and acquire the power to ıanipulate thought and wrest from it the extraordinary powers it holds. he book will also help them to attain refinement and culture by thought-iscipline, use their capacity for releasing wholesome, constructive and ıspiring thought-vibrations, obtain by accomplishing something great and rand, peace, happiness, and gain God-realization which is the meaning, m, and ultimate destiny of all human life on earth.

Chapter 1. Thought Power—Its Physics And Its Philosophy

Thought Excels Light in Speed

While light travels at the rate of 1,86,000 miles per second, thoughts virtually travel in no time.

Thought is finer than ether, the medium of electricity. In broadcasting, a singer sings beautiful songs at Calcutta. You can hear them nicely through the radio set in your own house at Delhi. All messages are received through the wireless.

Even so your mind is like a wireless machine. A saint with peace, poise, harmony and spiritual waves sends out into the world thoughts of harmony and peace. They travel with lightning speed in all directions and enter the minds of persons and produce in them also similar thoughts of harmony and peace. Whereas a worldly man whose mind is full of jealousy, revenge and hatred sends out discordant thoughts which enter the minds of thousands and stir in them similar thoughts of hatred and discord.

The Medium Through Which Thoughts Travel

If we throw a piece of stone in a tank or a pool of water, it will produce a succession of concentric waves travelling all around from the affected place.

The light of a candle will similarly give rise to waves of ethereal vibrations travelling in all directions from the candle.

In the same manner, when a thought, whether good or evil, crosses the mind of a person, it gives rise to vibrations in the Manas or mental atmosphere, which travel far and wide in all directions.

What is the possible medium through which thoughts can travel from one mind to another? The best possible explanation is that Manas or mind-substance fills all space like ether and it serves as the vehicle for thoughts, as Prana is the vehicle for feeling, as ether is the vehicle for heat, light and electricity and as air is the vehicle for sound.

The Ether of Space Registers Thoughts

You can move the world through thought-force. Thought has great ower. It can be transmitted from one man to another man. The powerful oughts of great sages and Rishis of yore are still recorded in the Akasa kasic records).

Yogins who have clairvoyant vision can perceive those thought-nages. They can read them.

You are surrounded by an ocean of thought. You are floating in the ean of thought. You are absorbing certain thoughts and repelling some in e thought-world.

Everyone has his own thought-world.

Thoughts Are Living Things

Thoughts are living things. A thought is as much solid as a piece of one. We may cease to be, but our thoughts can never die.

Every change in thought is accompanied by vibration of its matter nental). Thought as force needs a special kind of subtle matter in its orking.

The stronger the thoughts, the earlier the fructification. Thought is cussed and given a particular direction and, in the degree that thought is us focussed and given direction, it is effective in the work it is sent out to complish.

Thoughts Are Finer Forces

Thought is a finer force. This is supplied to us by food. If you read hhandogya Upanishad—the dialogue between Uddalaka and Svetaketu—u will understand this point well.

If the food is pure, thought also becomes pure. He who has pure oughts speaks very powerfully and produces deep impression on the inds of the hearers by his speech. He influences thousands of persons rough his pure thoughts.

A pure thought is sharper than the edge of a razor. Entertain always ire, sublime thoughts. Thought-culture is an exact science.

Thoughts As Wireless Messages

Those who harbour thoughts of hatred, jealousy, revenge and malice e verily very dangerous persons. They cause unrest and ill-will amongst en. Their thoughts and feelings are like wireless messages broadcast in her, and are received by those whose minds respond to such vibrations.

Thought moves with tremendous velocity. Those who entertain sublime and pious thoughts help others, who are in their vicinity and at a distance also.

Thoughts Are Tremendous Powers

Thought has got tremendous power. Thought can heal diseases. Thoughts can transform the mentality of persons. Thought can do anything. It can work wonders. The velocity of thought is unimaginable.

Thought is a dynamic force. It is caused by the vibrations of psychic Prana or Sukshma Prana on the mental substance. It is a force like gravitation, cohesion or repulsion. Thought travels or moves.

Thought-waves and Thought-transference

What is this world, after all? It is nothing but the materialization of the thought-forms of Hiranyagarbha or God.

You have got waves of heat and light and electricity in science. There are also thought-waves in Yoga. Thought has tremendous power. Everybody is experiencing the power of thought unconsciously to a greater or lesser degree.

Great Yogins like Jnanadev, Bhartrihari and Patanjali used to send and receive messages to and from distant persons through mind-telepathy (mental radio) and thought-transference. Telepathy was the first wireless telegraph and telephone service ever known to the world.

Just as you take physical exercises, play games such as tennis and cricket in order to maintain physical health, you will have to maintain mental health by radiating the right thought-waves, by taking Sattvic food, mental recreation of an innocent and harmless nature, change of mood, relaxation of mind by entertaining good, ennobling and sublime thoughts and by cultivating the habit of cheerfulness.

Marvels of Thought-vibrations

Every thought that you send out is a vibration which never perishes. It goes on vibrating every particle of the universe and if your thoughts are noble, holy and forcible, they set in vibration every sympathetic mind.

Unconsciously all people who are like you take the thought you have projected and in accordance with the capacity that they have, they send out similar thoughts. The result is that, without your knowledge of the consequences of your own work, you will be setting in motion great forces which will work together and put down the lowly and mean thoughts generated by the selfish and the wicked.

Diversity of Thought-vibrations

Every man has his own mental world, his own mode of thinking, his vn ways of understanding things and his own ways of acting.

Just as the face and voice of every man differ from those of another an, the mode of thinking and understanding also differs. That is the reason hy misunderstanding easily occurs between friends.

One is not able to understand rightly the views of another. Hence ction, rupture and quarrel occur within a minute even amongst fast ends. The friendship does not last long.

One should be in tune with the mental vibrations or thought-vibrations another. Then only can one easily understand another.

Lustful thoughts, thoughts of hatred, jealousy and selfishness produce storted images in the mind and cause clouding of understanding, rversion of intellect, loss of memory and confusion in the mind.

Conservation of Thought-energy

In physics you have the term 'power of orientation'. Though the mass of ergy is there, the current will not flow. It must be connected to the magnet d then the electric current will flow through the power of orientation.

Even so, the mental energy which is dissipated and misdirected in rious worthless worldly thoughts should be well directed in proper iritual channels.

Do not store in your brain useless information. Learn to unmind the ind. Unlearn whatever has been of no use to you. Then only can you fill ur mind with divine thoughts. You will gain new mental strength as the ssipated mental rays are collected now.

The Cell-theory and the Thoughts

A cell is a mass of protoplasm with a nucleus. It is endowed with telligence. Some cells secrete, while some cells excrete. The cells of the stes secrete semen; the cells of the kidneys excrete urine. Some cells act the rt of a soldier. They defend the body from the inroads or attacks of foreign isonous matter and germs. They digest and throw them out. Some cells rry food materials to the tissues and organs.

The cells perform their work without your conscious volition. Their tivities are controlled by the sympathetic nervous system. They are in rect communion with the mind in the brain.

Every impulse of the mind, every thought, is conveyed to the cells. ey are greatly influenced by the varying conditions or states of the mind. If there are confusion, depression and other negative emotions and thoughts in the mind, they are telegraphically transmitted through the nerves to every cell in the body. The soldier-cells become panic-stricken. They are weakened. They are not able to perform their function properly. They become inefficient.

Some people are extremely body-conscious, and possess no idea of the Self. They live irregular, indisciplined lives and fill their stomachs with sweets, pastries, and so on. There is no rest for the digestive and the eliminating organs. They suffer from physical weakness and diseases. The atoms, molecules and cells in their bodies produce discordant or inharmonious vibrations. They have no hope, confidence, faith, serenity and cheerfulness. They are unhappy. The life-force is not operating properly. Their vitality is at a low ebb. Their mind is filled with fear, despair, worry and anxiety.

Primal Thought and Modern Science

Thought is the greatest force on earth. Thought is the most powerful weapon in the armour of a Yogi. Constructive thought transforms, renews and builds.

The far-reaching possibilities of this force were most accurately developed to perfection by the ancients and put to the highest possible use.

For, thought is the primal force at the origin and back of all creation; the genesis of the entire phenomenal creation is given as a single thought that arose in the Cosmic Mind.

The world is the Primal Idea made manifest. This First Thought became manifest as a vibration issuing from the Eternal Stillness of the Divine Essence. This is the reference in classic terminology to the Ichha, desire of the Hiranyagarbha, Cosmic Soul, that originates as a Spandana or vibration.

This vibration is nothing like the rapid oscillation to and fro of physical particles, but is some thing infinitely subtle, so subtle as to be even inconceivable to the normal mind.

But this has made it clear that all forces are ultimately resolvable into a state of pure vibration. Modern science also has newly arrived at this conclusion after its prolonged researches in external physical nature.

Radium and the Rare Yogi

Radium is a rare commodity. Yogins who have controlled their thoughts are also very rare in this world, like radium.

Just as sweet perfume continuously emanates from an incense stick, so also divine perfume and divine effulgence (magnetic, Brahmic aura) radiate from a Yogi who has controlled his thoughts and who is constantly dwelling on Brahman or the Infinite.

The effulgence and perfume of his face is Brahma-Varchas. When you hold in your hand a bouquet made of jasmine, rose and Champaka flowers, the sweet perfume pervades the whole hall and tickles all alike.

Even so the perfume or fame and reputation (Yasas and Kirti) of a Yogi who has controlled his thoughts spreads far and wide. He becomes a cosmic force.

Thought—Its Weight, Size and Shape

Every thought has got weight, shape, size, form, colour, quality and power. A Yogi can see all these thoughts directly with his inner Yogic eye.

Thoughts are like things. Just as you hand over an orange to your friend and take it back, so also you can give a useful, powerful thought to your friend and also take it back.

Thought is a great force; it moves; it creates. You can work wonders with the power of thought. You must know the right technique of handling and manipulating a thought.

Thought—Its Form, Its Name and Colour

Suppose your mind is rendered perfectly calm, entirely without thoughts. Nevertheless, as soon as thought begins to rise, it will immediately take name and form.

Every thought has a certain name and a certain form. Thus you find that every idea that man has or can have, must be connected with a certain word as its counterpart.

Form is the grosser and name the finer state of a single manifesting power called thought.

But these three are one; wherever there is one, the other two also are there. Wherever name is, there are form and thought.

A spiritual thought has yellow colour. A thought charged with anger and hatred is of a dark red colour; a selfish thought has a brown colour and so on.

Thought—Its Power, Workings and Uses

Thought is a vital, living dynamic power—the most vital, subtle and irresistible force existing in the universe.

Through the instrumentality of thought you acquire creative power. Thought passes from one man to another. It influences people; a man of powerful thought can influence readily people of weak thoughts.

There are nowadays numerous books on thought-culture, thought power, thought-dynamics. A study of them will give you a comprehensive understanding of thought, its power, its workings and usefulness.

We Live in a Boundless World of Thoughts

Thought alone is the whole world, the great pains, the old age, death and the great sin, earth, water, fire, air, ether. Thought binds a man. He who has controlled his thoughts, is a veritable God on this earth.

You live in a world of thoughts. First is thought. Then there is the expression of that thought through the organ of speech. Thought and language are intimately connected. Thoughts of anger, bitterness and malice injure others. If the mind which is the cause of all thoughts vanishes, the external objects will disappear.

Thoughts are things. Sound, touch, form, taste and odour, the five sheaths, the waking, the dreaming and deep sleep states—all these are the products of mind. Sankalpa, passion, anger, bondage, time—know them to be the result of mind. Mind is the king of the Indriyas or senses. Thought is the root of all mental process.

The thoughts that we perceive all round us are only the mind in form or substance. Thought creates, thought destroys. Bitterness and sweetness do not lie in the objects, but they are in the mind, in the subject, in thinking. They are created by thought.

Through the play of the mind or thought upon objects, proximity appears to be a great distance and vice versa. All objects in this world are unconnected; they are connected and associated together only by thought, by the imagination of your mind. It is the mind that gives colour, shape, qualities to the objects. Mind assumes the shape of any object it intensely thinks upon.

Friend and enemy, virtue and vice are in the mind only. Every man creates a world of good and evil, pleasure and pain, out of his own imagination only. Good and evil, pleasure and pain do not proceed from objects. These belong to the attitude of your mind. There is nothing good nor pleasant in this world. Your imagination makes it so.

Thoughts, Electricity and Philosophy

Thoughts are giant-powers. They are more powerful than electricity. They control your life, mould your character, and shape your destiny.

Mark how one thought expands into many thoughts, within a short time. Suppose you get an idea to set up a tea-party for your friends. The one thought of 'tea' invites instantaneously the thoughts of sugar, milk, tea-cups, tables, chairs, table-cloth, napkins, spoons, cakes, biscuits, etc. So, this world is nothing but the expansion of thoughts. The expansion of thoughts of the mind towards the objects is bondage; and, the renunciation of thoughts is liberation.

You must be very watchful in nipping the thoughts in the bud. Only then will you be really happy. Mind tricks and plays. You must understand its nature, ways and habits. Then only can you control it very easily.

The world's most extraordinary book of practical philosophical idealism of India is *Yoga-Vasishtha*. The gist of this work is this: "The non-dual Brahman or the immortal soul alone exists. This universe as universe is not. Knowledge of the Self alone will free one from this round of births and deaths. Extinction of thoughts and Vasanas is Moksha. Expansion of mind alone is Sankalpa. Sankalpa or thought, through its power of differentiation generates this universe. This world is a play of the mind. This world does not exist in the three periods of time. Extinction of Sankalpas is Moksha. Annihilate this little 'I', Vasanas, Sankalpas, thoughts. Meditate on the Self and become a Jivanmukta."

Outer World Pre-exists in the Thoughts

Every thought has an image. A table is a mental image plus some external thing.

Whatever you see outside has its counterpart in the mind. The pupil is a small round thing in the eye. Retina is a small structure. How is it that the image of a big mountain seen through a small aperture or structure cast on the mind? This is a marvel of marvels.

The image of a mountain already exists in the mind. The mind is like a vast sheet of canvas that contains all the pictures of the objects seen outside.

World—A Projection of Thought

Careful reflection will show that the entire universe is in reality the projection of the human mind—*Manomatram Jagat*. Purification and control of the mind is the central aim of all Yogas. Mind in itself is but a record of impressions that keep expressing ceaselessly as impulses and thoughts. The mind is what it does. Thought impels you to action; activity creates fresh impressions in the mind-stuff.

Yoga strikes at the very root of this vicious circle by a method of effectively inhibiting the functions of the mind. Yoga checks, controls and stops the root function of the mind, i.e., *thought*. When thought is transcended, intuition functions and Self-knowledge supervenes.

Thought has the potency of creating or undoing the world in the twinkling of an eye. Mind creates the world according to its own Sankalpa or thought. It is the mind that creates this universe, (*Manomatram Jagat; Manahkalpitam Jagat*). Through the play of the mind, a Kalpa is reckoned by it as a moment and vice versa. Like a dream generating another dream in it the mind having no visible form generates existent visibles.

Thoughts, World and the Timeless Reality

It is the mind that is the root cause of the tree of Samsara with its thousands of shoots, branches, tender leaves and fruits. If you annihilate thoughts, you can destroy the tree of Samsara at once.

Destroy the thoughts as soon as they arise. The root will dry up through the annihilation of thoughts, and the tree of Samsara will wither soon.

This demands considerable patience and perseverance. You will be bathed in the ocean of bliss when all thoughts are extirpated. This state is indescribable. You will have to feel it yourself.

Just as the fire is absorbed into its source when the fuel is burnt out, so also, the mind is absorbed into its source, the Atman, when all Sankalpas or thoughts are annihilated. Then one attains Kaivalya, the experience of the Timeless Reality, the state of absolute independence.

Chapter 2. Thought Power—Its Laws And Its Dynamics

Thought—The Architect of Destiny

If the mind dwells continually upon one train of thought, a groove is formed into which the thought-force runs automatically and such a habit of thought survives death and since it belongs to the ego, is carried over to the subsequent earth-life as a thought-tendency and capacity.

Every thought, it must be remembered, has got its own mental image. The essence of the various mental images formed in one particular physical life is being worked out in the mental plane. It constitutes the basis for the next physical life.

Just as a new physical body is formed in every birth, so also a new mind and a new Buddhi are formed in every birth.

Not easy is the act of explaining the detailed workings of thought and destiny. Every Karma produces twofold effect, one on the individual mind and the other on the world. Man makes the circumstances of his future life by the effect of his actions upon others.

Every action has a past which leads up to it; every action has a future which proceeds from it. An action implies a desire which prompted it and a thought which shaped it.

Each thought is a link in an endless chain of causes and effects, each effect becoming a cause and each cause having been an effect; and each link in the endless chain is welded out of three components—desire, thought and activity. A desire stimulates a thought; a thought embodies itself as an act. Act constitutes the web of destiny.

Selfish coveting of the possessions of others, though never carried out into active cheating in the present, makes one a thief in a later earth-life, while hatred and revenge secretly cherished are the seeds from which the murderer springs.

So again, unselfish loving yields as harvest the philanthropist and the saint; and every thought of compassion helps to build the tender and pitiful nature which belongs to one who is a friend to all creatures.

Sage Vasishtha asks Rama to do Purushartha, or show the prowess of self-exertion. Do not yield to fatalism. It will induce inertia and laziness. Recognize the Great Powers of Thought. Exert. By right thinking make for yourself a great destiny.

Prarabdha is Purushartha of last birth. You sow an action and reap a habit; a habit sown results in character. You sow a character and reap a destiny.

Man is the master of his own destiny. You yourself make, by the power of your thought, your destiny. You can undo it if you like. All faculties, energies and powers are latent in you. Unfold them, and become free and great.

Thoughts Chisel Your Countenance

Your face is like a gramophone record or plate. Whatever you think is at once written on your face.

Every vicious thought serves as a chisel or needle to write down the thoughts on your countenance. Your faces are covered with the scars and wounds which are made by the vicious thoughts of hatred, anger, lust, jealousy, revenge, etc.

From the nature of the scar on your face, we can at once read your state of mind. We can at once diagnose the disease of your mind.

He who thinks that he can hide his thoughts is a dunce of the first water. His position is like that of the ostrich which, when chased by the hunters, hides its head underneath the sand and imagines that it cannot be seen by anyone.

Face is the index of the mind. Face is the mould of the mind. Every thought cuts a groove in the face. A divine thought brightens the face. An evil thought darkens the face. Continued divine thoughts increase the aura or halo.

Continued evil thoughts increase the depth of dark impressions, just as the continued striking of a vessel against the edge of a well while drawing water makes deeper and deeper hollow on the vessel. The facial expression truly advertises the inner state of the mind or the true contents of the mind.

The face is like an advertisement-board wherein is advertised what is going inside the mind. Your thoughts, sentiments, modes and emotions produce their strong impressions on the face.

In your face, you can hardly hide your thoughts. You may wrongly think that you have kept up your thoughts in secret. The thoughts of lust, greed, jealousy, anger, revenge, hatred, etc., at once produce their deep impressions on your face.

The face is a faithful recorder and a sensitive registering apparatus to register and record all the thoughts that are in your mind.

The face is a polished mirror to indicate the nature of the mind and its contents at a particular time.

Thoughts Feature the Physical Expressions

Mind is the subtle form of this physical body. The physical body is the outward manifestation of the thoughts. So when the mind is wrought, the body is wrought too.

As a man of rough appearance generally cannot invoke love and mercy of others, so a rough-minded man cannot invoke love and mercy of anybody.

Mind very conspicuously reflects on the face its various states which a man of intelligence can very easily read.

The body follows the mind. If the mind thinks of falling from a height, the body prepares itself immediately and shows external signs. Fear, anxiety, grief, cheerfulness, hilarity, anger, all produce their various impressions on the face.

Your Eyes Betray Your Thoughts

The eyes which represent the windows of the soul bespeak of the condition and state of the mind.

There is a telegraphic instrument in the eyes to transmit the messages or thoughts of treachery, depression, gloom, hatred, cheerfulness, peace, harmony, health, power, strength and beauty.

If you have the faculty to read the eyes of others, you can read the mind at once. You can read the uppermost thought or dominant thought of a man if you are careful to mark the signs in his face, conversation and behaviour. It needs a little pluck, acumen, training, intelligence and experience.

Negative Thoughts Poison Life

Thoughts of worry and thoughts of fear are fearful forces within us. They poison the very sources of life and destroy the harmony, the running efficiency, the vitality and vigour. While the opposite thoughts of cheerfulness, joy and courage, heal, soothe, instead of irritating, and immensely augment efficiency and multiply the mental powers. Be always cheerful. Smile. Laugh.

Psycho-physical Imbalances

Thought exerts its influence over the body. Grief in the mind weakens the body. Body influences the mind also in its turn. A healthy body makes the mind healthy. If the body is sick, the mind also becomes sick. If the body is strong and healthy, the mind also becomes healthy and strong.

Violent fits of hot-temper do serious damage to the brain cells, throw poisonous chemical products into the blood, produce general shock and depression and suppress the secretion of gastric juice, bile and other digestive juices in the alimentary canal, drain away your energy, vitality, induce premature old age and shorten life.

When you are angry, the mind becomes disturbed. Similarly, when the mind is disturbed, the body also becomes disturbed. The whole nervous system is agitated. You become enervated. Control anger by love. Anger is a powerful energy that is uncontrollable by practical Vyavaharic Buddhi, but controllable by pure reason (Sattvic Buddhi) or Viveka-Vichara.

The Creative Powers of Thought

Thought creates the world. Thought brings things into existence. Thoughts develop the desires and excite the passions. So, the contrary thoughts of killing the desires and passions will counteract the former idea of satisfying the desires. So when a person is impressed with this, a contrary thought will help him to destroy his desires and passions.

Think of a person as a good friend of yours and there the thing is created as a reality. Think of him as your foe, then also the mind perfects the thought into an actuality. He who knows the workings of the mind and has controlled it by practice is really happy.

Similar Thoughts Attract Each Other

In the thought-world also, the great law "Like attracts like", operates. People of similar thoughts are attracted towards each other. That is the reason why the maxims run as follows: "Birds of the same feather flock together," "A man is known by the company he keeps."

A doctor is drawn towards a doctor. A poet has attraction for another poet. A songster loves another songster. A philosopher likes another philosopher. A vagabond likes a vagabond. The mind has got a 'drawing power'.

You are continually attracting towards you, from both the seen and the unseen sides of life-forces, thoughts, influences and conditions most akin to those of your own thoughts and lines.

In the realm of thought, people of similar thoughts are attracted to one another. This universal law is continually operating whether we are conscious of it or not.

Carry any kind of thought you please about with you and so long as you retain it, no matter how you roam over the land or sea, you will unceasingly attract to yourself, knowingly or inadvertently, exactly and only what corresponds to your own dominant quality of thought. Thoughts are your private property and you can regulate them to suit your taste entirely by steadily recognizing your ability to do so.

You have entirely in your own hands to determine the order of thought you entertain and consequently the order of influence you attract and are not mere willowy creatures of circumstances, unless indeed you choose to be.

Spanish Flu and the Contagion of Thoughts

Mental actions are real actions. Thought is the real action; it is a dynamic force. It may be remembered, thought is very contagious; nay, more contagious than the Spanish Flu.

A sympathetic thought in you raises a sympathetic thought in others with whom you come in contact. A thought of anger produces a similar vibration in those who surround an angry man. It leaves the brain of one man and enters the brains of others who live at a long distance and excites them.

A cheerful thought in you produces cheerful thoughts in others. You are filled with joy and intense delight when you see a batch of hilarious children playing mirthfully and dancing in joy.

A thought of joy in us creates sympathetically a thought of joy in others. So do sublime elevating thoughts.

Keep a good and honest man in the company of a thief. He will begin to steal. Keep a sober man in the company of a drunkard. He will begin to drink. Thought is very contagious.

The Application of a Psychological Law

Keep the heart young. Do not think: "I have become old." To think "I have become old" is a bad habit. Do not entertain this thought. At 60, think "I am 16." As you think, so you become. This is a great psychological law.

"As a man thinketh so he becometh." This is a great truth or truism. Think, "I am strong," strong you become. Think, "I am weak," weak you become. Think, "I am a fool," fool you become. Think, "I am a sage or God," sage or God you become.

Thought alone shapes and moulds a man. Man lives always in a world of thoughts. Every man has his own thought-world.

Imagination works wonders. Thought has tremendous force. Thought as already said, is a solid thing. Your present is the result of your past thoughts and your future will be according to your present thoughts. If you think rightly, you will speak rightly and act rightly. Speech and action simply follow the thoughts.

Understand the Laws of Thought

Every man should have a comprehensive understanding of the laws of thought and their operations. Then alone can one live in this world smoothly and happily. He can utilize the helping forces to serve his ends in the best possible manner.

He can neutralize the hostile forces or antagonistic currents. Just as the fish swims against the current, so also he will be able to go against the hostile currents by adjusting himself properly and safeguarding through suitable precautionary methods.

Otherwise he becomes a slave. He is tossed about hither and thither helplessly by various currents. He is drifted like a wooden plank in a river. He is very miserable and unhappy always, although he is wealthy and possesses everything.

The captain of a steamer who has mariner's compass, who has knowledge of the sea, the routes and the oceanic currents can sail smoothly. Otherwise his steamer will be drifted here and there helplessly and wrecked by dashing against some icebergs or rocks. Likewise, a wise sailor in the ocean of this life who has a detailed knowledge of the Laws of Thought and Nature can sail smoothly and reach the goal of his life positively.

Understanding the laws of Thought, you can mould or shape your character in any way you like. The common saying, "As a man thinketh so he becometh," is one of the great laws of Thought. Think you are pure, pure you will become. Think you are noble, noble you will become.

Become an embodiment of good nature. Think good of all. Do always good actions. Serve, love, give. Make others happy. Live to serve others. Then you will reap happiness. You will get favourable circumstances or opportunities and environments.

If you hurt others, if you do scandal-mongering, mischief-mongering, backbiting, talebearing, if you exploit others, if you acquire the property of others by foul means, if you do any action that can give pain to others, you will reap pain. You will get unfavourable circumstances or opportunities and environments.

This is the law of thought and nature. Just as you can build your good or bad character by sublime or base thinking, so also you can shape your favourable or unfavourable circumstances by doing good or bad actions.

A man of discrimination is always careful, vigilant and circumspect. He always watches carefully his thoughts. He introspects.

He knows what is going on in his mental factory what Vritti or Guna is prevailing at a particular time. He never allows any evil thought to enter the gates of his mental factory. He at once nips them in the bud.

By his good thinking, by watching the nature of his thoughts, by introspection, by active noble thinking, the man of discrimination builds his noble character, forms his high destiny. He is careful in his speeches. He speaks little. He speaks sweet loving words. He never utters any kind of harsh words that can affect the feelings of others.

He develops patience, mercy and universal love. He tries to speak truth. Thus he puts a check on the Vak-Indriya and the impulses of speech. He uses measured words. He writes measured lines. This produces deeply profound and favourable impression on the minds of the people.

He practices Ahimsa and Brahmacharya in thought, word and deed. He practices Saucha and Arjava (straightforwardness). He tries to keep up balance of mind and to be always cheerful. He keeps up Suddha-Bhava. He tries these three kinds of Tapas (physical, verbal and mental), and controls his actions. He cannot think any evil. He cannot do any evil action.

He prepares himself to get always favourable circumstances. He who spreads happiness will always get such favourable circumstances as can bring him happiness. He who spreads pain to others will, doubtless, get according to the law of thought such unfavourable circumstances as can bring him misery and pain. Therefore, man creates his own character and circumstances, by the manner of his own thinking.

Bad character can be transmuted into good one, by good thoughts, and unfavourable circumstances can be changed into favourable circumstances by doing good actions.

The Laws Implied in Higher Thoughts

As you think, so you become. As are your thoughts so must be your life. Improve your thinking. Better thoughts bring better actions.

Mere thinking of the objects of this world is pain. Bondage is caused by the very act of thought. Pure thought is a mightier force than electricity.

The mind which is attracted by objects of sense, tends to bondage, while that which is not so attracted tends to emancipation. Mind is a dacoit.

Slay this mind-dacoit. You will be happy and free for ever. Manifest all your strength in the task of conquering your mind. This is true manliness or Purushartha.

Self-denial is a means to the purification and refinement of mind. Purify and still the thoughts. The layers of ignorance covering knowledge, will not be removed without a calm mind.

The subtle part of food forms the mind. Mind is manufactured out of food. The subtle part of food is transformed into mind. Food does not mean merely what we eat, but what we gather through all our senses.

Learn to see God everywhere. This is real food for the eye. Purity of thought depends upon purity of food. You can see better, hear better, taste better, think better, when you entertain sublime divine thoughts.

Look at an object through a green or red glass; the object appears green or red. Even so, the objects are coloured by the desires through the mirror-mind. All mental states are transitory; they produce pain and sorrow.

Have freedom of thought. Free yourself from the slavery of prejudice that blunts intellect and dulls thoughts. Think of the immortal Atman. This is the right method of direct, original thinking. The Atman reveals Itself after the purification of thoughts. When the mind is serene without any want, without any motive, without any craving or desire or thought, without any compulsion, without hope, then the supreme Atman shines. There is the experience of Bliss. Live the way in which saints live. This is the only way to victory over thoughts, mind and the lower self and until you have conquered mind, there can be no sure and permanent victory.

Thought—A Boomerang

Be careful of your thoughts. Whatever you send out of your mind, comes back to you. Every thought you think, is a boomerang.

If you hate another, hate will come back to you. If you love others, love will come back to you.

An evil thought is thrice cursed. First, it harms the thinker by doing injury to his mental body. Secondly, it harms the person who is its object. Lastly, it harms all mankind by vitiating the whole mental atmosphere.

Every evil thought is as a sword drawn on the person to whom it is directed. If you entertain thoughts of hatred, you are really a murderer of that man against whom you foster thoughts of hatred. You are your own suicide, because these thoughts rebound upon you only.

A mind tenanted by evil thoughts acts as a magnet to attract like thoughts from others and thus intensifies the original evil.

Evil thoughts thrown into the mental atmosphere poison receptive minds. To dwell on an evil thought gradually deprives it of its repulsiveness and impels the thinker to perform an action which embodies it.

Thoughts and the Waves of the Sea

Thoughts are like the waves of an ocean. They are countless. You may become desperate in the beginning of your attempt to conquer them.

Some thoughts will subside while some other thoughts will gush out like a stream. The same old thoughts that were once suppressed may again show their faces after some time. Never become despondent at any stage of practice. You will surely get inner spiritual strength. You are bound to succeed in the end. All the Yogins of yore had to encounter the same difficulties that you are experiencing now.

The process of destruction of mental modifications is difficult and long. All thoughts cannot be destroyed in a day or two. You should not give up the practice of destroying the thoughts in the middle when you come across some difficulties or stumbling blocks.

Your first attempt should be to reduce your wants and desires. Reduce your wants and desires; then, the thoughts will decrease by themselves. Gradually all thoughts will be extirpated.

Colour and Influence of Saintly Thoughts

The Buddha declared, "All that we are is made up of our thoughts." It is our thoughts that cause the round of births. So, we should always strive to purify our thoughts.

When we go and sit near a sage, we feel a unique calmness; but if we are in the company of a bad and selfish person, we feel uneasy. It is because the vibrations of peace and calmness emanate from the aura of the sage, whereas from the aura of the selfish person emanate vibrations of evil and selfish thoughts.

The second effect of thought is the creation of a definite form. The quality and the nature of a thought determine, the colour and the clearness of that thought-form. A thought-form is a living entity and it has a strong tendency to carry out the intention of the thinker. Blue thought-forms denote devotion.

The thought-form of self-renunciation is of the lovliest pale azure with a white light shining through it. Thought-forms of selfishness, pride and anger are of grey-brown, orange and red colour, respectively.

We are always surrounded by these thought-forms and our minds are seriously affected by them. Not one-fourth of our thoughts are our own, but are simply picked up from the atmosphere. Mostly they are of evil nature. So we should always utter God's name mentally. It will always protect us from their evil influence.

Aura and Dynamics of a Developed Mind

Particularly around minds of highly developed thought power, we sense the manifest phenomenon of a powerful aura.

The palpable influence of a highly developed mind over a less developed mind, needs to be specially marked. It is not possible to provide a description of what it is like to be in the presence of a Master, or a developed adept.

To sit in his presence, though he hardly speaks a word, is to feel a thrilling sensation and discover the impacts of new inspirations that it wields on our minds.

Mind carries aura—mental aura or psychic aura. The Sanskrit term for aura is Tejas. It is brilliance or halo that emanates from the phenomenon of mind. In those who have sought the full development of their minds, we find it extremely effulgent. It is capacitated to travel long distances and affect in the most beneficial manner a large number of persons who are privileged to come under its influence. It must be noted that the spiritual aura is far more powerful than either psychic or Pranic or mental aura.

Dynamics of Thoughts and Moods

People of gloomy moods attract to themselves, gloomy things and gloomy thoughts from others and from the Akasic records in the physical ether.

Persons with hope, confidence and cheerful spirits attract thoughts of similar nature from others. They are always successful in their attempts.

People with negative moods of depression, anger, and hatred do positive injury to others. They infect others and raise these destructive Vrittis in others. They are culpable. They do great damage in the thought-world.

People with happy and cheerful moods are a blessing to society. They bring happiness to others.

Just as a young, beautiful lady covers her face and does not like to come out to mix with others in society when she has a nasty festering sore on her cheeks or nose, also you should not come in public and mix with your friends and other people when you have a mood of depression, a mood of hatred or jealousy. For, you will infect others with these moods. You will be a menace to the society.

Thought-dynamics in Universal Environs

Thought actually leaves the brain and hovers about. When a thought, whether good or evil, leaves the mind of a person it gives rise to vibrations in the Manas or mental atmosphere, which travel far and wide in all directions.

It enters the brains of others also. A sage living in a Himalayan cave transmits a powerful thought to a corner of America. He who tries to purify himself in a cave, really purifies the world, helps the world at large. Nobody can prevent his pure thoughts coming out and passing on to those others that really want them.

Just as the sun goes on continuously converting into vapour every drop of water that is on the surface of the earth and just as all the vapour thus rising up gathers together in the form of clouds, all the thoughts that you project from your own lonely corner will mount up and be wafted across space, join similar thoughts projected by those who are like you and, in the end, all these holy thoughts will come down with tremendous force to subjugate undesirable forces.

Chapter 3. Value And Uses Of Thought Power

Serve Others by Thought-vibrations

A true monk or Sannyasin can do everything through his thought-vibrations. A Sannyasin or Yogi need not become the President of an Association or the leader of a social or political movement. It is a foolish and puerile idea.

Indians have now imbibed the missionary spirit of the West and cry out that Sannyasins should come out and take part in social and political activities. It is a sad mistake.

It is not necessary that a Sannyasin, a saint should appear on the platform to help the world, to preach and elevate the minds of people.

Some saints preach by example. Their very lives are an embodiment of teaching. Their very sight elevates the minds of thousands.

A saint is a living assurance for others for God-realization. Many draw inspiration from the sight of holy saints.

No one can check the thought-vibrations from the saints. Their pure, strong thought-vibrations travel a very long distance, purify the world and enter the minds of many thousands of persons. There is no doubt in this.

Doctors Can Heal by Suggestion

Doctors should have a thorough knowledge of the science of suggestion. Sincere, sympathetic doctors are very rare. Doctors who have no knowledge of suggestion do more harm than good. They kill patients sometimes by unnecessarily frightening them.

If there is a little cough of an ordinary nature, the doctor says: "Now, my friend, you have got T.B. You must go to Bhowali or Switzerland or Vienna. You must go in for a course of tuberculin injection." Poor patient is frightened. There is not at all any sign of consumption. The case is an ordinary one. It is simple catarrh of the chest from exposure to chills. The patient actually develops phthisis by fright and worry owing to the wrong destructive suggestion of the doctor.

The doctor ought to have told him: "Oh, it is nothing. It is simple cold. You will be all right by tomorrow. Take a purgative and inhale a little oil of eucalyptus. Adjust your diet. It is better you fast today." Such doctor is God Himself. He must be adored.

A doctor may say now: "Well, sir, if I say so, I will lose my practice. I cannot pull on in this world." This is a mistake. Truth always gains victory. People will run to you as you are sympathetic and kind. You will have a roaring practice.

There is healing by suggestion. This is a drugless treatment. This is suggestive therapeutics. By good and powerful suggestion, you can cure any disease. You will have to learn this science and practice it. All doctors of Homeopathic, Allopathic, Ayurvedic and Unani systems should know this science. They can combine this system along with their own systems. They will have a roaring practice by this happy combination.

Yogins Preach by Thought-transference

Through their spiritual vibrations and magnetic aura the unknown real Yogins help the world more than the 'Yogins' of the platform. Preaching from the pulpits and platforms belongs to men of second grade spirituality, who have no knowledge and never put to use the supernormal faculties and powers latent in them.

Great adepts and Mahatmas transmit their message through telepathy to deserving aspirants in different corners of the world. Means of communication that are supernormal to us are quite normal to a Yogi.

Influence Others by Thought

You can influence another man without any audible language. What is wanted is concentration of thought that is directed by the will. This is telepathy.

Here is an exercise for your practice in telepathy. Think of your friend or cousin who is living in a distant land. Bring a clear-cut image of his face to your mind. If you have his photo, look at it and speak to it audibly. When you retire to bed think of the picture with intense concentration. He will write to you the desired letter the following day or so. Try this yourself. Do not doubt. You will be quite surprised.

You will get success and firm conviction in the science of telepathy. Sometimes, when you are writing something or reading a newspaper, suddenly you get a message from some one near and dear to you. You think of him suddenly. He has sent a message to you. He has thought of you seriously.

Thought-vibrations travel faster than light or electricity. In such instances, the subconscious mind receives the messages or impressions and transmits the same to the conscious mind.

Varied Utility of Thought Power

The science of thought power is very interesting and subtle. This thought-world is more real relatively than this physical universe.

The power of thought is very great. Every thought of yours has a literal value to you in every possible way. The strength of your body, the strength of your mind, your success in life and the pleasures you give to others by your company – all depend on the nature and quality of your thoughts. You must know thought-culture, and develop thought power.

Powers of Thought—Their Value

If you have a comprehensive understanding of the workings of the thought-vibrations, if you know the technique of controlling the thoughts, if you know the method of transmitting beneficial thoughts to others at a distance by forming clear-cut well-defined powerful thought-waves, you can use this thought power a thousandfold more effectively. Thought works wonders.

A wrong thought binds. A right thought liberates. Therefore, think rightly and attain freedom. Unfold the occult powers hidden within you by understanding and realizing the powers of the mind. Close your eyes. Slowly concentrate. You can see distant objects, hear distant sounds, send messages to any part not only of this world, but of the other planets as well, heal persons thousands of miles off from you and move about to distant places in no time.

Believe in the powers of the mind. Interest, attention, will, faith and concentration will bring the desired fruit. Remember that mind is born of the Atman through His Maya or Illusory Power.

Thoughts Accomplish Many a Mission

You can aid a friend in trouble by transmitting to him thoughts of comfort, right from the place where you are. You can help a friend in search of Truth by thoughts, clear and definite of the truths you know.

You can send into the mental atmosphere thoughts which will raise, purify and inspire all who are sensible to them.

If you send out a loving, helpful thought to another man, it leaves your brain, goes directly to that man, raises a similar thought of love in his mind and returns back to you with redoubled force.

If you send out a thought of hatred to another man, it hurts that man and hurts you also by turning back to you with redoubled force.

Therefore, understand the laws of thought, raise only thoughts of mercy, love and kindness from your mind and be happy always.

When you send out a useful thought to help others, it must have a definite, positive purpose and aim. Then only it will bring out the desired effect. Then only that thought will accomplish a definite work.

Power of Thoughts That Prompt

Gain a clear understanding of suggestions and their effects upon the mind. You should be careful in the use of suggestions. Never give wrong suggestion which will have destructive results to anybody. You will be doing a great harm and a disservice to him. Think well before you speak.

Teachers and professors should have a thorough knowledge of the science of suggestion and auto-suggestion. They can educate and elevate students in an efficient manner.

In Southern India, when children cry out in houses parents frighten them by saying: "Look here, Balu! Irendukannạn (the two-eyed man) has come. Keep quiet, or I will hand you over to this man." "Puchandi (or ghost) has come," and suggestions of this sort are very destructive. The child becomes timid.

The minds of children are elastic, tender and pliable. Samskaras are indelibly impressed at this age. Changing or obliterating the Samskaras becomes impossible when they grow. When the child grows into a man, he manifests timidity.

Parents should infuse courage into the minds of their children. They should say: "Here is a lion. See the lion in this picture. Roar like a lion. Be courageous. See the picture of Shivaji, Arjuna or Clive. Become chivalrous."

In the West, teachers show the pictures of battlefields to children and say: "Look here, James! See this picture of Napoleon. Look at his chivalry. Won't you like to become a Commander-in-chief of the army or a Brigadier-General?" They infuse courage into the minds of children from their very childhood. When they grow, these Samskaras get strengthened by additional external stimuli.

Practice Thought-transference

Practice telepathy in the beginning from a short distance. It is better to practice at night, to start with.

Ask your friend to have the receptive attitude and concentration at ten o'clock. Ask him to sit on Vajrasana or Padmasana with closed eyes in a dark room.

Try to send your message exactly at the appointed time. Concentrate on the thoughts that you want to send. Will strongly now. The thoughts will leave your brain and enter the brain of your friend.

There may be some mistakes in the beginning here and there. When you advance in practice and know the technique well, you will always be correct in sending and receiving messages.

Later on, you will be able to forward messages to different corners of the world. Thought-waves vary in intensity and force. The sender and receiver should practice great and intense concentration. Then there will be force in sending the messages, clarity and accuracy in receiving the messages. Practice in the beginning telepathy from one room to the next room in the same house.

This science is very pleasant and interesting. It needs patient practice. Brahmacharya is very essential.

Parapsychology and Subconscious Thoughts

Even as the sacred Ganga takes its origin in Gangotri, Himalayas, and runs perennially towards Ganga Sagar, the thought-currents take their origin from the bed of Samskaras (impressions) in the inner layers of the mind, wherein are embedded the Vasanas or latent subtle desires, and flow incessantly towards the objects both in waking state and in dreaming state. Even a railway engine, is sent to the engine-shed for rest, when its wheels become overhot; but this mysterious engine of mind goes on thinking without a moment's rest.

Practice of telepathy, thought-reading, hypnotism, mesmerism and psychic healing clearly proves that the mind exists and that a higher mind can influence and subjugate the lower mind. From the automatic writing and the experiences of a hypnotized person, we can clearly infer the existence of the subconscious mind which operates throughout the twenty-four hours. Through spiritual Sadhana change the subconscious thoughts and mind and become a new being.

Power of Vigorous, Divine Thoughts

Thought is life. What you think, that you are. Your thought creates your environment. Your thoughts constitute your world.

If you entertain healthy thoughts, you can keep good health. If you hold on to sickly thoughts in the mind, thoughts of diseased tissues, thoughts of weak nerves, thoughts of improper functioning of organs, of viscera, you can never expect good health, beauty and harmony.

Remember that body is a product of the mind and is under the control of mind.

If you hold on to vigorous thoughts, your body, too, will be vigorous. Thoughts of love, peace, contentment, purity, perfection, Divinity, will make you, and also others around you, perfect and Divine. Cultivate divine thoughts.

Chapter 4. The Functions Of Thought Power

Thoughts Promote Radiant Health

The body is internally associated with the mind, rather the body is a counterpart of the mind; it is a gross visible form of the subtle, invisible mind. If there is pain in the tooth or in the stomach or in the ear, the mind is at once affected. It ceases to think properly; it is agitated, disturbed and perturbed.

If there is depression in the mind, the body also cannot function properly. The pains which afflict the body are called the secondary diseases, *Vyadhi*, while the Vasanas or desires that afflict the mind are termed mental or primary diseases, *Adhi*.

Mental health is more important than physical health. If the mind is healthy, the body will necessarily be healthy. If the mind is pure, if your thoughts are pure, you will be free from all diseases primary and secondary. "*Mens sana in corpore sano*—a sound mind in a sound body."

Thoughts Develop Personality

A sublime thought elevates the mind and expands the heart; a base thought excites the mind and renders the feelings morbid and dark.

Those who have even a little control over their thoughts and speech will have a calm, serene, beautiful, charming face, a sweet voice and their eyes will turn brilliant and lustrous.

Thoughts Affect the Body

Every thought or emotion or word produces a strong vibration in every cell of the body and leaves a strong impression there.

If you know the method of raising an opposite thought, then you can lead a happy harmonious life of peace and power. Thought of love will at once neutralize a thought of hatred. A thought of courage will immediately serve as a powerful antidote against a thought of fear.

Thought Power Changes Destiny

Man sows a thought and reaps an action. He sows an action and reaps a habit. He sows a habit and reaps a character. He sows a character and reaps a destiny.

Man has made his own destiny by his own thinking and acting. He can change his destiny. He is the master of his own destiny. There is no doubt of this. By right thinking and strong exertion, he can become the master of his destiny.

Some ignorant people say: "Karma does everything. It is all destiny. If I am destined by my Karma to be like this or that why then should I exert? It is my destiny only."

This is fatalism. This will bring inertia, stagnation and misery. This is perfect misunderstanding of the laws of Karma. This is a fallacious argument. An intelligent man will certainly not put such a question. You have made your own destiny from within by your thoughts and actions.

You have a free will to choose now. You have got Svatantrata in action. A rogue is not an eternal rogue for all times. Put him in the company of a saint. He will change in no time. He will think and act now in a different way and will change his destiny. He will become saintly in character.

Dacoit Ratnakar was changed into Sage Valmiki. Jagai and Madai were transformed. They were rogues of the first waters. You can become a Yogi or a Jnani. You can make your destiny. You can make your Karma in any way you like. Use the Power of Thought. Think rightly, think nobly. You will have only to think, and to act. By right thinking, by right desiring, by right acting, you can become a Sage, a millionaire. You can attain the position of Indra or Brahma by good thought and action, by good Karma. Man is not a helpless being. He has a free will of his own.

Thoughts Cause Physiological Disorders

Every change in thought makes a vibration in your mental body and this when transmitted to the physical body causes activity in the nervous matter of your brain. This activity in the nervous cells causes many electrical and chemical changes in them. It is thought-activity which causes these changes.

Intense passion, hatred, long-standing bitter jealousy, corroding anxiety, fits of hot temper actually destroy the cells of the body and induce diseases of the heart, liver, kidneys, spleen and stomach.

It is a point worthy to note with care that every cell in the body suffers or grows, receives a life impulse or a death impulse, from every thought that enters the mind, for you tend to grow into the image of that which you think about most.

When the mind is turned to a particular thought and dwells on it, a definite vibration of matter is set up and often, more of this vibration is caused, the more does it tend to repeat itself to become a habit, to become automatic. The body follows the mind and imitates its changes. If you concentrate your thought the eyes become fixed.

Thought Power Creates Environments

It is often said that man is the result of his environmental forces. This is not true. We cannot believe this, because the facts always prove the contrary. Many of the world's greatest men have been born in poverty and in adverse circumstances.

Many who have been born in the slums and filthy surroundings have risen to the highest status in the world. They have won laurels of fame and distinguished themselves in politics, literature and poetry. They have become brilliant geniuses and beacon-lights of the world. How do you account for this?

Sri T. Mutthuswamy Aiyar, the first Indian High Court Judge in Madras was born in absolute poverty. He had to study at night under municipal lanterns. He had not sufficient food. He was clad in rags. He struggled hard and achieved greatness. He rose above the environmental forces by his strong will-power and iron-determination.

In the West, sons of cobblers and fishermen have risen to very high position. Boys who did polishing of boots in the streets and who were selling beer in bars and were cooking in hotels have become famous poets and able journalists.

Johnson was placed in quite adverse environments. Goldsmith was "passing rich with 40 pounds a year." Sir Walter Scott was very poor. He had no place to live in. The life of James Ramsay Macdonald is worth mentioning. He was a man of great Purushartha. He rose from poverty to power—from the field of labour to the status of Prime Minister of Britain. His first job was addressing envelopes for 10 Shillings a week.

He was too poor to buy tea; so he drank water instead. His main meal every day for months was a three-penny beef-steak pudding. He was a pupil-teacher. He took great interest in Politics and Science. He was a journalist. He gradually through right exertion (Purushartha) rose to the position of a Prime Minister.

Sri Sankaracharya, the exponent of Advaita philosophy, a spiritual giant and a brilliant genius was born in poor, unfavourable environments and circumstances. There are thousand and one instances like these. It is quite obvious, therefore, that unfavourable environments cannot annihilate the potential greatness and excellence of the future geniuses and that one can outgrow environments by diligent application, patience, perseverance, truthfulness, honesty, integrity, sincerity of purpose, iron-will and strong determination.

Every man is born with his Samskaras. The mind is not a *tabula rasa* or a blank sheet of paper. It contains the impressions of thoughts and actions of the previous births. Samskaras are the latent potentialities. These good Samskaras are valuable assets for man. Even though he is placed in unfavourable environments, these Samskaras give him protection from extraneous, undesirable, hostile influences. They help his growth and evolution.

Miss not any opportunity. Avail yourself of all opportunities. Every opportunity is meant for your uplift and development. If you see a sick man lying down on the roadside in a helpless condition, take him on your shoulders or vehicle to the nearest hospital. Nurse him. Give him hot milk or tea or coffee. Shampoo his legs with Divine Bhava.

Feel the all-pervading, all-permeating, interpenetrating indwelling God in him. See divinity in the glow in his eyes, in his cry, in his breath, in his pulsation and motion of his lungs.

God has given this opportunity for you to develop mercy and love, to purify your heart and to remove Ghrina, hatred and jealousy. Sometimes if you are very timid, God will place you in such circumstances wherein you will be forced to exhibit courage and presence of mind by risking your life. These world figures who have risen to eminence have utilized all opportunities to the best advantage. God shapes the minds of human beings by giving them opportunities.

Remember that in your weakness lies the strength, because you will be always on your alert to safeguard yourself. Poverty has got its own virtues. Poverty infuses humility, strength, power of endurance and luxury begets laziness, pride, weakness, inertia and all sorts of evil habits.

Do not grumble, therefore, of bad environments. Create your own mental world and environments. That man who tries to evolve or grow in adverse environments will be a very strong man indeed. Nothing can shake him. He will be of a sterner stuff. He will have strong nerves.

Man is certainly not a creature of environments or circumstances. He can control and modify them by his capacities, character, thoughts, good actions and right exertion (Purushartha). Tivra (intense) Purushartha can change the destiny. That is the reason why Vasishtha and Bhishma have placed Purushartha above destiny. Therefore, dear brothers! Exert. Conquer nature and rejoice in the eternal Satchidananda Atman.

Thoughts Form the Physical Body

The body with its organs is no other than the thought. The mind contemplating upon the body becomes the body itself, and then enmeshed in it, is afflicted by it.

This physical body is the mould as it were, made by the mind for its own enjoyment, for its outpouring of energy and thereby gaining different experiences of this world through the five avenues or channels of knowledge, the five Jnana-Indriyas (organs of knowledge or perception). The body is really our thoughts, moods, convictions and emotions objectified, made visible to the naked eyes.

All the bodies have their seat in the mind only. Without water can a garden exist?

It is the mind which transacts all business and is the highest of bodies. Should this gross body be dissolved, the mind will assume fresh bodies to its liking very quickly. Should the mind be paralyzed, then the body will not evince our intelligence.

With the majority of mankind, the thought is greatly under the control of the body. Their minds being very little developed, they live in Annamaya Kosa, mostly. Develop the Vijnanamaya Kosa and through Vijnanamaya Kosa (Buddhi) control the Manomaya Kosa (mind).

The erroneous thought that you are the body is the root of all evils. Through wrong thinking you identify yourself with the body. Dehadhyasa arises. You are attached to the body. This is Abhimana. Then Mamata (mine-ness) arises. You identify yourself with your wife, children, house, etc. It is identification or attachment that brings about bondage, misery and pain.

Chapter 5. The Development Of Thought Power

Acquisition of Thought Power by Moral Purity

A man who speaks the truth and has moral purity has always powerful thoughts. One who has controlled anger by long practice has tremendous thought power.

If a Yogi whose thought is very powerful speaks one word, it will produce tremendous impression on the minds of others.

Virtues like truthfulness, earnestness and industry are the best sources of mental power. Purity leads to wisdom and immortality. Purity is of two kinds, internal or mental and external or physical.

Mental purity is more important. Physical purity is also needed. With the establishment of internal mental purity, cheerfulness of mind, one-pointed mind, conquest of Indriyas and fitness for the realization of the Self are obtained.

Thought Power by Concentration

There is no limit to the power of human thought. The more concentrated the human mind is, the more power is brought to bear on one point.

The rays of the mind are scattered in the case of the worldly-minded persons. There is dissipation of mental energy in various directions. For purposes of concentration, these scattered rays have to be gathered by the practice of concentration and then the mind must be made to turn towards God.

Cultivate attention, you will have good concentration. A serene mind is fit for concentration. Keep the mind serene. Be cheerful always. Then alone can you concentrate. Be regular in your concentration. Sit in the same place, at the same time, 4 a.m.

Celibacy, Pranayama, reduction of wants and activities, dispassion, silence, seclusion, discipline of the senses, Japa, control of anger, giving up reading novels, newspapers and visiting cinemas are all aids to concentration.

Too much physical exertion, too much talking, too much eating, too much mixing with worldly persons, too much walking, too much sexual indulgence, are obstacles to concentration.

Thought Power by Organized Thinking

Destroy random thinking. Take a subject and think of its different aspects and bearing. When you think so on one subject, never allow any other thought to enter the conscious mind. Withdraw the mind again to the subject on hand.

Take for instance, you begin to think on the life and teachings of Jagadguru Adi Sankaracharya. Think of his birthplace, his early life, his character, his personality, his virtues, his teachings, his writings, his philosophy, some of the important utterings of his works or Slokas, the Siddhis that he exhibited from time to time, his Digvijaya, his four disciples, his four Mutts, his commentary on the Gita, the Upanishads and the Brahma Sutras. Think of these items one by one in order. Exhaust them. Again and again, bring the mind to the point. Then take up another subject.

By this practice, you will develop organized thinking. The mental images will gain intense strength and force. They will become clear-cut and well-defined. In ordinary persons the mental images are distorted and undefined.

Thought Power by Will-power

Every sensual thought rejected, every temptation resisted, every harsh word withheld, every noble aspiration encouraged, helps you to develop will-power or soul-force and takes you nearer and nearer to the Goal.

With strong feeling, repeat mentally: "My will is powerful, pure and irresistible. OM OM OM. I can do everything through my will. OM OM OM. I have an invincible will. OM OM OM."

Will is the dynamic soul-force. When it operates all the mental powers such as the power of judgment, power of memory, power of grasping, power of conversation, reasoning power, power of discrimination, power of reflection and inference—all these come into instant play.

Will is the king of mental powers. When rendered pure and irresistible, thought and will can work wonders. Will becomes impure and weak through vulgar passions, love of pleasures and desires. The lesser the number of desires, the stronger is the thought power, and the will. When sexual energy, the muscular energy, anger, etc., are transmuted into the will-force they are controlled. There is nothing impossible on earth for a man of strong will-power.

When you give up an old habit of drinking coffee, you have controlled to a certain extent the sense of taste, destroyed one Vasana, and have eliminated the craving for it. As there is freedom from the efforts to procure coffee and also from the habit of taking it, you will gain some peace. The energy involved in the hankering for coffee, and which was agitating you, will now be converted into the power of will. By this conquest over one desire, you gain will-power; and if you conquer some fifteen such desires, your will-power will be fifteen times stronger and more powerful. And this conquest, by imparting strength to the will, will help you conquer other desires, too.

Unruffled state of the mind, poise, cheerfulness, inner strength, capacity to turn out difficult works, success in all undertakings, power to influence people, a magnetic and dynamic personality, magnetic aura on the face, sparkling eyes, steady gaze, powerful voice, magnanimous gait, unyielding nature, fearlessness, etc., are some of the signs or symptoms that indicate that one's will is growing.

Simple Prescriptions for Clear Thinking

The mental images of the common man are generally very distorted. He does not know what deep thinking is. His thoughts run riot. There is a great deal of confusion in his mind, sometimes.

It is only thinkers, philosophers and Yogins who have well-defined, clear-cut, mental images. They can be seen through clairvoyance very vividly. Those who practice concentration and meditation develop strong, well-formed mental images.

Most of your thoughts are not well-grounded. They come and slip away. They are, therefore, vague and indefinite. The images are not clear, strong and well-defined.

You will have to reinforce them by clear, continuous and deep thinking. Through Vichara, ratiocination, Manana or deep reflection and meditation, you will have to make the thoughts settle down and crystallize into a definite shape. Then the philosophical idea will become firm.

Through right thinking, reasoning, introspection and meditation, you will have to clarify your ideas. Then confusion will vanish. The thoughts will get settled and well-grounded.

Think clearly. Clarify your ideas again and again. Introspect in solitude. Purify your thoughts to a considerable degree. Silence the thoughts.

Don't allow the mind to bubble. Let one thought-wave rise and settle down calmly. Then allow another thought to enter. Drive off all extraneous thoughts that have no connection with the subject-matter you are handling at the present moment.

Sadhana for Deep and Original Thinking

Most of us do not know what right thinking is. Thinking is shallow in the vast majority of persons. Deep thinking is given to few. Thinkers are very few in this world.

Deep thinking needs intense Sadhana (practice). It takes innumerable births for the proper evolution of the mind. Then only can it think deeply and properly.

Independent and original thinking is resorted to by the Vedantins. Vedantic Sadhana (Manana, reflection) demands a sharp intellect.

Hard thinking, persistent thinking, clear thinking, thinking to the roots of problems, to the very fundamentals of the situation, to the very presuppositions of all thoughts and being is the very essence of Vedantic Sadhana.

You will have to abandon an old idea, however strong and ingrained it may be, when you get a new elevating idea in its stead.

If you have no courage to face the results of your thinking, to swallow the conclusions of your thinking, whatever they may mean to you personally, you should never take the trouble to philosophize. Take up to devotion.

Meditation for Applied and Sustained Thinking

Being a great force, thought carries tremendous power. It becomes a matter of great moment to know how to use this power in the highest possible way and to the greatest possible effect. This can best be done by the practice of meditation.

Applied thinking applies the mind to the object and sustained thinking keeps it continually engaged; rapture brings about the expanding and bliss of the developing mind whose motives for non-distraction have been accomplished by those two kinds of thinking.

Meditation can arise when applied and sustained thinking, rapture, bliss and collectedness of mind arise.

Acquire Creative Thought Power

Thought is a vital living force—the most vital, subtle and irresistible force that exists in the universe.

Thoughts are living things; they move; they possess form, shape, colour, quality, substance, power and weight.

Thought is the real action; it reveals itself as a dynamic force.

A thought of joy creates sympathetically a thought of joy in others. The birth of a noble thought is a potent antidote to counteract an evil thought.

Through the instrumentality of exercised positive thought, we come to acquire creative power.

Develop Individuality: Resist Suggestions

Do not be easily influenced by the suggestions of others. Have your own sense of individuality. A strong suggestion, though it does not influence the subject immediately, will operate in due course. It will never go in vain.

We all live in a world of suggestions. Our character is daily modified unconsciously by association with others.

We unconsciously imitate the actions of those whom we admire. We daily absorb the suggestions of those with whom we come in daily contact. We are acted upon by these suggestions. A man of weak mind yields to the suggestions of a man of strong mind.

The servant is always under the influence of the suggestions of his master. The wife is under the influence of the suggestions of her husband. The patient is under the influence of the suggestions of the doctor. The student is under the influence of the teacher.

Custom is nothing but the product of suggestion. The dress that you put on, the manners, the behaviour and even the food that you eat are all the outcome of suggestions only.

Nature suggests in various ways. The running rivers, the shining sun, fragrant flowers, the growing trees, are all incessantly sending you suggestions.

Supernormal Powers by Thought-discipline

A powerful occultist hypnotizes the whole audience collectively through his power of concentration and will and performs the rope-trick. He throws a red rope in the air, gives suggestion to the onlookers that he will climb in the air through this rope and disappears from the platform in the twinkling of an eye. But nothing is recorded when a photograph is taken.

Understand and realize the powers of thought. Unfold the hidden powers or occult faculties. Close the eyes. Concentrate. Explore the higher regions of the mind.

You can see distant objects, hear distant voices, send messages to distant places, heal persons who are at a distance and move about to a distant place in the twinkling of an eye.

Chapter 6. Thoughts—Their Varieties And Their Conquest

Get Over Gloomy Thoughts

Very carefully watch all your thoughts. Suppose you are assailed by gloomy thoughts. You experience depression. Take a small cup of milk or tea. Sit calmly. Close your eyes. Find out the cause for the depression and try to remove the cause.

The best method to overcome the gloomy thoughts and the consequent depression, is to think of inspiring thoughts and inspiring things. Remember again, positive overcomes negative. This is a grand effective law of nature.

Now think strongly of the opposite thoughts, the opposite of gloom. Think of those things that elevate your mind; think of cheerfulness. Imagine the advantage of cheerfulness. Feel that you are in actual possession of this quality.

Again and again repeat the formula: OM CHEERFULNES, mentally. Feel, "I am very cheerful." Begin to smile and laugh several times.

Sing: sometimes this can elevate you quickly. Singing is very beneficial to drive off gloom. Chant OM loudly several times. Run in the open air. The depression will vanish soon. This is the *Pratipaksha Bhavana* method of Raja Yogins. This is the easiest method.

The method of driving gloom by force—by willing, by assertions, by command—taxes the 'will' very much although it is the most efficient. It demands great strength of will. Ordinary people will not succeed. The method of displacing or dislocating the negative feeling by substituting the opposite, positive feeling, is very easy. Within a very short time, the undesirable feeling vanishes. Practice this and feel. Even if you fail several times, continue. You will be successful after some sittings and some practice.

You can treat in the same manner other negative thoughts and feelings as well. If there is the feeling of anger think of love. If there are thoughts of jealousy, think of the advantages of charitableness and magnanimity. If there are thoughts of gloom, then think of some inspiring scenery that you saw sometime ago, or recall to mind some inspiring passage.

If there is harshness of heart, think of mercy. If there is lust, think of the advantage of celibacy. If there is dishonesty, think of honesty, integrity. If there is miserliness, think of generosity and generous persons.

If there is infatuation or Moha, think of discrimination and Atmic Vichara; if there is pride, think of humility. If there is hypocrisy, think of frankness and its invaluable advantages. If there is jealousy, think of nobility and magnanimity. If there is timidity, think of courage, and so on.

You will drive off the negative thoughts and feelings and will be established in a positive state. Practice of a continued type is essential. Be careful in the selection of your companions. Talk very little and that, too, on useful matters.

Victory Over Intrusive Thoughts

In the beginning of your practice of thought-control you will experience great difficulty. You will have to wage war with them. They will struggle their level best for their own existence. They will say, "We have every right to remain in this palace of mind. We have a sole monopoly from time immemorial to occupy this area. Why should we vacate our dominion now? We will fight for our birthright till the end."

They will pounce upon you with great ferocity. When you sit for meditation only, all sorts of evil thoughts will crop up. As you attempt to suppress them they want to attack you with redoubled force and vigour. But positive always overcomes the negative.

Just as darkness cannot stand before the sun, just as the leopard cannot stand before the lion so also all these dark negative thoughts—these invisible intruders, enemies of peace—cannot stand before the sublime divine thoughts. They must die by themselves.

Drive Away Obnoxious Thoughts

Drive away from your mind all unnecessary, useless and obnoxious thoughts. Useless thoughts impede your spiritual growth; obnoxious thoughts are stumbling blocks to spiritual advancement.

You are away from God when you entertain useless thoughts. Substitute thoughts of God. Entertain only thoughts that are helpful and useful. Useful thoughts are the stepping-stones to spiritual growth and progress.

Do not allow the mind to run into the old grooves and to have its own ways and habits. Be on the careful watch.

If a pebble in our boot torments us, we expel it. We take off the boot and shake it out. Once the matter is fairly understood, it is just as easy to expel an intruding and obnoxious thought from the mind. About this there ought to be no doubt, no two opinions. The thing is obvious, clear and unmistakable.

It should be as easy to expel an obnoxious thought from your mind as it is to shake a stone out of your shoe; and, till a man can do that, it is just nonsense to talk about his ascendancy and conquest over nature. He is a mere slave and prey to the bat-winged phantoms that flit through the corridor of his brain.

Master Worldly Thoughts

Worldly thoughts will trouble you a lot in the beginning of your new life of thought-culture. They trouble you, also when you take to the practice of meditation and spiritual life. But, if you are regular in your cultivation of spiritual thoughts and in your meditation, these worldly thoughts will gradually die by themselves.

Meditation is a fire to burn these thoughts. Do not try to drive all worldly thoughts. Entertain positive thoughts concerning the object of your meditation. Positively think of the lofty things.

Watch your mind always very carefully. Be vigilant. Be on the alert. Do not allow waves of irritability, jealousy, anger, hatred, lust, to rise from the mind. These dark waves and worldly thoughts are enemies of meditation, peace and wisdom.

Conquer them immediately by entertaining sublime divine thoughts. Worldly thoughts that have arisen may be destroyed by originating good thoughts and maintaining them by repeating any Mantra or the Name of the Lord, by thinking on any form of the Lord, by practice of Pranayama, by singing the Name of the Lord, by doing good actions, by thinking on the misery that arises from the worldly thoughts.

When you attain a state of purity, no worldly thoughts will take their rise in your mind. Just as it is easy to check the intruder or enemy at the gate, so also it is easy to overcome a worldly thought as soon as it rises. Nip it in the bud. Do not allow it to strike a deep root.

Conquer Impure Thoughts

When you are very busy in your daily work, you may not harbour any impure thought; but when you take rest and leave the mind blank, the impure thoughts will try to enter insidiously. You must be careful when the mind is relaxed.

Thoughts gain strength by repetition. If you entertain an impure thought or good thought once, this impure thought or good thought has a tendency to recur again.

Thoughts crowd together just as the birds of the same feather flock together. So also, if you entertain one impure thought all sorts of impure thoughts join together and attack you. If you entertain any good thought, all good thoughts join together to help you.

Subdue Negative Thoughts

Learn to subdue, to purify, to order all your thoughts. Fight against all negative thoughts and doubts. Let sublime divine thoughts come to you from every side.

Thoughts of depression, failure, weakness, darkness, doubts, fear, etc., are negative thoughts. Cultivate positive thoughts of strength, confidence, courage, cheerfulness. The negative thoughts will disappear.

Fill the mind with divine thoughts, by Japa, Prayer, Dhyana and study of holy books. Be indifferent to all negative and undivine thoughts. They will pass away. Do not struggle with them. Pray to God for strength. Read the lives of saints. Study the Bhagavata and the Ramayana. All devotees have passed through similar ordeals. So, take heart.

Overcome Habitual Thoughts

All sorts of habitual thoughts, concerning the body, the dress, the food, and so on, must be overcome through the Atma-Chintana, or reflection on the Nature of the divine Self within one's own Heart. This is an uphill work. It demands patient, incessant practice and inner spiritual strength.

Srutis emphatically declare: "This Atman cannot be obtained by weak persons." Sincere aspirants dedicate their whole being to contemplation of the Eternal, having withdrawn their affection from the world of sense-objects.

Those who have destroyed the Vasanas and host of habitual thoughts will enjoy their final beatitude in the Brahmic seat, replete with trust, quiescence and equality. They will have equal vision over all. This mischievous and powerful mind generates all pains and all fears, all sorts of diversities, heterogeneity, distinctions and dualities and destroys all noble, spiritual wealth. Slay this troublesome mind.

When the seen and the sight merge into one another in the seer, then is the experience of Ananda (bliss). This is Turiya state. Then one sees the illimitable Jnana, Atman only everywhere. All sorts of distinctions and dualities vanish now entirely.

Thoughts of attraction, and thoughts of repulsion, likes and dislikes, Raga-Dvesha are annihilated *in toto*. Then the sage will not be conscious of the existence of the body, though working in it. He will never lose his control even amidst the many illusions of the world, like a woman who performs her household duties whilst her mind is engrossed in her paramour at a distance. The sage will always centre his mind on Brahman.

May you always be performing only those virtuous actions that will help you in the attainment of Jnana, without any thought of worldly prosperity in the future. May you live drowned in the ocean of Brahmic Delight, in a state of full illumination, having destroyed all dualities, distinctions and differences!

Triumph Over Unimportant Thoughts

Do not try to drive away the unimportant and irrelevant thoughts. The more you try, the more they will return, the more they will gain strength. You will tax your energy and will.

Become indifferent. Fill the mind with divine thoughts. They will gradually vanish. Get yourself established in Nirvikalpa Samadhi through constant meditation.

Removal of tension in the muscles of the body brings repose and calmness to the mind. By relaxation you give rest to the mind, tired nerves and the overworked muscles. You will get immense peace of mind, strength and vigour. When you practice relaxation of either body or mind, the brain should not be occupied with various sorts of loose extraneous thoughts. Anger, disappointment, failure, indisposition, misery, sorrow, quarrels cause internal mental strain. Expel them.

Transform Instinctive Thoughts

Thinking is of four kinds, viz., symbolic thinking, instinctive thinking, impulsive thinking and habitual thinking.

Thinking through words is symbolic thinking. Instincts are more powerful than impulses. Thoughts of body, food, drink, bath, etc., are habitual thinking.

You can stop easily symbolic thinking. It is difficult to stop instinctive and impulsive thinking.

Mental poise and calmness may be brought about by the eradication of worry and anger. Fear really underlies both worry and anger. Be careful and thoughtful. All unnecessary worries should be avoided. Think of courage, joy, bliss, peace and cheerfulness. Sit for fifteen minutes in a relaxed state in an easy comfortable position.

You can lie on an easy-chair. Close your eyes. Withdraw the mind from outside objects. Still the mind. Silence the bubbling thoughts.

Lessen the Number of Habitual Thoughts

Generally, in untrained persons, four or five kinds of thoughts occupy the mind at a time. Household thoughts, business thoughts, thoughts of office, thoughts of body, thoughts of food and drink, hope and anticipation, some kind of planning to get money, some kind of thoughts of revenge, some habitual thoughts of answering calls of nature, bathing, etc., occupy the mind at a time.

When you are studying a book with interest at 3.30 p.m. the idea of pleasure of witnessing a cricket match at 4 p.m. disturbs your study every now and then. It is only a Yogi with one-pointed mind, who can have only one thought at a time and can keep it as long as he likes.

If you watch the mind carefully, you will find that many thoughts are inconsistent. The mind wanders at random aimlessly. There will be some thoughts of the body and its wants, some thoughts of friends, some thoughts of acquiring money, some thoughts of eating and drinking, some thoughts of your boyhood, etc.

If you can study the mind and if you have consistent thoughts of one subject or one kind only to the exclusion of all other thoughts, this itself is a very great achievement, is a great step in advancement in thought-control. Do not be discouraged.

Gather Inspirational Thoughts

The goal of life is the attainment of divine consciousness. This goal is the realization that you are neither this perishable body nor that changing and finite mind, but you are all-pure, ever-free Atman.

Remember always this inspiring thought—*Ajo-Nityah Sasvatoyam Purano*: Unborn, Eternal, Permanent is this Ancient One. This is your real nature. You are not this little passing personality hooked on to a name and form. You are not Ramaswamy or Mukherji or Mehta or Matthew or Garde or Apte. You have only fallen into this little delusion by an accident through some passing cloud of ignorance. Awake and realize that you are Pure Atman.

There is another wonderful Upanishadic inspirational thought. It is *Isavasyamidam Sarvam*: every content of the universe is throbbing with the Life of the Lord. Smile with the flowers and the green grass. Smile with the shrubs, ferns and twigs. Develop friendship with all neighbours, dogs, cats, cows, human beings, trees, in fact, with all nature's creations. You will have a perfect and rich life.

Reflect Over Illuminating Thoughts

If you want to develop your thought power, if you want to build up your personality and become great, always keep with you some books of inspiring and illuminating thoughts. Read them over and over again, until they become part of your daily action and living.

Here is a list of some illuminating thoughts, for reflection:

1. A clean conscience makes a stout heart and a strong mind.

2. Poverty is the elder brother of laziness.

3. Knowledge of the Self is the greatest treasure. Meditation is the key to knowledge.

Right Thoughts for Wrong Thoughts

Thoughts of passion and lust, should be conquered by an earnest practice of Brahmacharya, by intense aspiration to realize the Truth, to know God, by meditating on the great advantages of purity.

Thoughts of hatred and anger should be controlled by generating thoughts of love, forgiveness, mercy, friendliness, peace, patience and non-violence.

Pride and thoughts connected with pride must be controlled by a systematic mental examination of the value of cultivating humility.

Thoughts of greed, grabbing and possessiveness should be dispelled by pursuit of honesty, disinterestedness, generosity, contentment and non-covetousness.

Nobility and magnanimity, complacency and greatness of heart, will help you get over all thoughts of narrowness, jealousy, meanness.

Delusion and infatuation are best conquered by the development of discrimination. Vanity is overcome by a many-sided simplicity, arrogance by politeness.

The Gamut of Thoughts

There are various kinds of thoughts. There are instinctive thoughts. There are visual thoughts. There are auditory thoughts (thinking in terms of hearing). There are symbolic thoughts (thinking in terms of symbols). Some thoughts are habitual.

There are kinesthetic thoughts (thinking in terms of movement, as in playing a game). There are emotional thoughts. Thoughts change from the visual stage to auditory stage and from auditory to kinesthetic.

There is intimate connection between thinking and respiration as there is close relation between mind and Prana. When the mind is concentrated, breathing becomes slow. If one thinks fast the respiration also becomes fast. There is a thought-reading machine known as psychograph which registers correctly the type of thoughts.

Mean Thoughts and Moral Development

Uncontrolled thoughts are the roots of all evils. Each thought by itself is extremely weak, because the mind is generally distracted by countless and ever-varying thoughts.

The more the thoughts are restrained, the more is the mind concentrated, and consequently the more does it gain in strength and power.

It demands patient work to destroy mean and base thoughts; but the entertainment of sublime thoughts is the easiest and rapid method of destroying base thoughts. Ignorant of the laws of thoughts, the worldly-minded individual falls a prey to all sorts of thoughts—thoughts of hatred, anger, revenge, lust—and grows weak-willed, deficient in powers of discernment, and slave of the adverse subtle workings of the mind.

The best method of gaining mental power is by entertaining sublime, noble and good thoughts and through their aid controlling the dissipative, distractive, diversifying, worldly and base thoughts.

When all evil thought harasses the mind, the best method of conquering it is by ignoring it. How can we ignore an evil thought? By forgetting it. How can we forget? By not indulging in it again, and also by not brooding over it.

How can we prevent the mind from indulging in it again or brooding over it? By thinking of something very interesting, something sublime and inspiring. Ignore, forget, think of something inspiring; these three constitute the great Sadhana for establishing mastery over evil thoughts.

Chapter 7. Positive Methods For Thought-Control

Thought-control by Practice of Concentration

Silence the bubbling thoughts. Calm the surging emotions. Concentrate on a concrete form in the beginning. Concentrate on a flower, on the form of Lord Buddha, on any dream picture, on the effulgent light of the heart, on the picture of any saint, or your Ishta Devata.

Have three or four sittings; early morning, 8 a.m., 4 p.m. and 8 p.m. Devotees concentrate on the heart, Raja Yogins on Trikuti (the seat of the mind), Vedantins on the Absolute. Trikuti is the space between the eyebrows.

You can also concentrate on the tip of the nose, the naval, or the Muladhara (below the last vertebra of the spinal column).

When irrelevant thoughts enter the mind, be indifferent. They will pass away. Do not drive them forcibly. They will persist and resist. It will tax your will. They will enter with redoubled force. But substitute divine thoughts. Irrelevant thoughts will gradually fade out. Be slow and steady in the practice of concentration.

Concentration is practiced for stopping the modification of the mind. Concentration is holding the mind to one form or object for a long time. To remove the tossing of the mind and various other obstacles which stand in the way of one-pointedness, the practice of concentration on one thing alone should be made.

Concentration is opposed to sensuous thoughts and desires, bliss to flurry and worry, sustained thinking to perplexity, applied thinking to sloth and torpor, rapture to ill-will.

It is easy to concentrate the mind on external objects. The mind has a natural tendency to go outwards. Keep the picture of Sri Krishna, Rama, Narayana, Devi or Lord Jesus or any picture, in front of you. Look at it steadily without winking. Gaze at the head, then at the body, then at the legs. Repeat the same process again and again. When your mind calms down look at a particular spot only, then close the eyes and mentally visualize the picture.

You should be able to visualize the picture very clearly even in its absence. You will have to call up the mental picture at a moment's notice. Keep it there steadily for sometime. This is concentration. You will have to practice this daily.

If you want to increase your power of concentration, you will have to reduce your worldly desires and activities. You will have to observe silence everyday for some hours. Then only can the mind concentrate very easily and without difficulty.

In concentration you will have only one thought or wave in the mind-lake. The mind assumes the form of only one object. All other operations of the mind are suspended.

Thought-control by a Positive Attitude

Try to acquire the power of closing yourself against detrimental or undesirable thoughts and influences by making yourself positive by a particular attitude of the mind. By so doing, you may be receptive to all higher impulses of the soul within and to all higher forces and influences from without. Make a suggestion to yourself, "I close myself; I make myself positive to all things below and open and receptive to all higher influences, to all things above." By taking this attitude of the mind, consciously, now and then, it soon becomes a habit.

All the lower and undesirable influences from both the seen and the unseen sides of life are closed out while all higher influences are invited and, in the degree that they are invited, they will enter.

In the mind there is doubt; there is reality also. A doubt arises whether there is a God or not. This is termed Samsaya-Bhavana. Another doubt crops up whether I can realize Brahman or not. Then another voice tells: "God or Brahman is real. He is a solid, concrete Reality as an Amalaka fruit in my hand. He is a mass of knowledge and Ananda (Prajnanaghana, Chidghana, Anandaghana). I can realize!"

We have clearly understood something and these ideas are well-grounded and ingrained. Some ideas are hazy and not firm. They come and go. We will have to cultivate ideas and ground them till they are firmly fixed and implanted. Clarification of ideas will remove perplexity and confusion in the mind. When a doubt arises, "Whether there is God or not, whether I will succeed in Self-realization or not," it must be dispelled by well-directed suggestions and affirmations such as: "It is true; I will succeed. There is no doubt of this." "In my dictionary, in my vocabulary, there are no such words, as 'can't', 'impossible', 'difficult', etc. Every thing is possible under the sun." Nothing is difficult when you strongly make up your mind. Strong determination and firm resolution will bring sanguine success in every affair or undertaking, and particularly so in the conquest of mind.

Thought-control by Non-cooperation

Non-cooperate with the mind in its evil wanderings. Gradually the mind will come under your control. Here is the practical method to non-cooperate with the mind. If the mind says: "I must eat today sweetmeats," say unto the mind: "I will not cooperate with you today. I will not eat sweetmeats. I will eat only bread and Dal." If the mind says: "I must go to cinema," say unto the mind: "I will attend the Satsanga of Swami Ramananda and hear his discourses on the Upanishads." If the mind says: "I must wear a silk shirt," say unto the mind: "I will not wear in future any silk clothing; I will wear only Khaddar." This is the method to non-cooperate with the mind. Non-cooperation with the mind is swimming against the sensual currents. The mind will be thinned out and gradually it will become your obedient servant. You will gain mastery over the mind.

The self-controlled man, moving among the objects with senses under restraint and free from attraction and repulsion, attains to peace. The mind and the senses are naturally endowed with the two currents of attraction and repulsion. Therefore, the mind and the senses like certain objects and dislike certain other objects. But the disciplined man moves among the sense-objects with a mind and senses free from attraction and repulsion, mastered by Self, and attains the peace of the Eternal.

The disciplined self has a very strong will. Therefore, the senses and mind obey his will. The disciplined self takes only those objects which are quite necessary for the maintenance of the body without any love or hatred. He never takes those objects which are forbidden by the Sastras.

Art of Thinning Out Thoughts

In the rubber plantations, planters take recourse to the method of thinning out the rubber trees by cutting the small surplus trees which stand in the vicinity of big trees. By so doing they can tap more milk (rubber juice) from the big trees. Even so, you must thin out the thoughts by destroying them one by one in order to drink the ambrosial milk or nectar of immortality.

Just as you retain only the good fruits from the basket and discard the bad ones, so also, keep good thoughts in your mind and reject evil ones.

Just as the warrior chops off the heads of enemies, one by one, when they come out of a fortress through a trap door, so also, chop off the thoughts, one by one, when they emerge out through the trap door to the surface of the mind.

When the tail of a lizard is cut, the cut end will flutter about for sometime as there is still a little residual Prana in the tail. After one or two minutes all motion will cease. Even so, even after thinning and reducing the thoughts, some thoughts will move about like the tail of the lizard. But they are powerless. They cannot do any serious harm. There is no vitality in them.

Just as the drowning man tries to catch anything to save himself, so also, these lifeless thoughts try their level best to come back to their previous state of life and vigour. If you go on regularly with your daily practice of concentration and meditation, they will die by themselves like a gheeless lamp.

Passion, egoism, jealousy, pride and hatred are very deep-rooted. If you cut the branches of a tree, they grow again after sometime. Even so, these thoughts that are suppressed or thinned out for sometime, manifest again after sometime. They should be completely rooted out by strenuous efforts, Vichara, meditation, etc.

Thought-control by Napoleon's Method

When you think on one subject, do not allow other thoughts to enter. When you think of a rose, think of the different kinds of roses only. Do not allow other thoughts to enter.

When you think of mercy, think of mercy and mercy only. Do not think of forgiveness and tolerance. When you study the Gita, do not think of tea or a cricket match. Be wholly occupied with the subject on hand.

Napoleon controlled his thoughts in this manner: "When I want to think of things more pleasant, I close the cupboards of my mind revealing the more unpleasant things of life, and open up the cupboards containing the more pleasant thoughts. If I want to sleep, I close up all the cupboards of mind!"

Arrest the Recurrence of Evil Thoughts

Suppose the evil thoughts stay in your mind for twelve hours and recur every third day. If you can make them stay for ten hours and recur once in a week by daily practice of concentration and meditation, that is a decided improvement. If you continue your practice, the period of stay and recurrences will be gradually lessened.

Eventually they will disappear altogether. Compare your present state of mind with that of last year or year before last. You will be able to find out your progress.

The progress will be very slow in the beginning. It will be difficult for you to gauge your growth and progress.

Give the Wrong Thought No Concession

At first a wrong thought enters the mind. Then you entertain a strong imagination. You take delight in dwelling on that wrong thought.

You give consent to its stay in the mind, and gradually the wrong thought, when it is not resisted, takes a strong hold in your mind.

Then it becomes very difficult to drive it off. The proverb goes: "Give a rogue an inch and he will take an ell." This is true of wrong thoughts also.

Nip the Bad Thought in Its Bud

Just as you close your door or gate when a dog or an ass tries to come in, so also, close your mind before any evil thought can enter and produce an impression on your physical brain. You will become wise soon and attain eternal, infinite peace and bliss.

Wipe out lust, greed and egoism. Entertain only pure holy thoughts. This is an uphill task, a difficult task. You will have to practice it. You will succeed in your attempt after sometime.

Destruction of one bad thought will give you strength to annihilate other thoughts and will develop your soul-force or will-power.

Never despair though you may fail in crushing a bad thought. No pains, no gains. Inner spiritual strength will gradually manifest in you. You can feel this.

Spiritual Practice for Elimination of Evil Thoughts

Your mind will sometimes shudder when evil thoughts enter your mind. This is a sign of your spiritual progress. You are growing spiritually. You will be much tormented when you think of your evil actions committed in the past.

This is also a sign of your spiritual upheaval. You will not repeat now the same actions. Your mind will tremble. Your body will quiver whenever a wrong thought of some evil action urges you to do the same act through force of habit. Continue your meditation with full vigour and earnestness. All memories of evil actions, all evil thoughts, all evil promptings of Satan, will die by themselves. You will be established in perfect purity and peace.

In the beginning all sorts of evil thoughts will arise in your mind as soon as you sit for meditation. Why does this happen during meditation, when you attempt to entertain pure thoughts?

Aspirants leave their spiritual practice of meditation on account of this. If you try to drive a monkey, it attempts to pounce upon you in vengeance. Even so, the old evil thoughts try to attack you revengefully and with redoubled force at the time when you try to raise good, divine thoughts. Your enemy endeavours to resist you vehemently when you try to eject him out of your house.

There is a law of resistance in nature. The old evil thoughts assert and say, "O man! Do not be cruel. You have allowed us to stay in your mental factory from time immemorial. We have every right to abide here. We have helped you upto this time in all your evil actions. Why do you want to oust us from our dwelling place? We will not vacate our abode." Do not be discouraged. Go on with your practice of meditation regularly. These evil thoughts will be thinned out.

Eventually they will all perish. Positive always overcomes negative. This is the law of nature. Negative evil thoughts cannot stand before positive good thoughts. Courage overcomes fear. Patience overcomes anger and irritability. Love overcomes hatred. Purity overcomes lust.

The very fact that you feel uneasy now when an evil thought comes to the surface of the mind during meditation indicates that you are growing in spirituality.

In the past you consciously harboured all sorts of evil thoughts. You welcomed and nourished them. Persist in your spiritual practices. Be tenacious and diligent. You are bound to succeed. Even a dull type of aspirant will notice a marvellous change in him if he keeps up the practice of Japa and meditation for 2 or 3 years in a continuous stream. Now he cannot leave the practice. Even if he stops his practice of meditation for a day, he will actually feel that he has lost something on that day. His mind will be quite uneasy.

Best Remedies for Evil Thoughts

When the mind is vacant, evil thoughts try to enter. Evil thinking is the beginning or starting point of adultery. Through a lustful look only, you have already committed adultery in the heart. Mental actions are the real actions. Remember this! God judges a man by his motives; worldly people judge a man by his external physical actions. You will have to look to the motive of the man. Then you will not be mistaken.

Keep the mind fully occupied. Then evil thoughts will not enter. An idle brain is the devil's workshop. Watch the mind every minute.

Always engage yourself in some work—stitching, cleaning vessels, sweeping, drawing water, reading, meditating, counting the beads, singing divine songs, praying, serving the elders or nursing the sick. Avoid loose talk and gossip. Fill the mind with sublime thoughts, such as those contained in the Gita, the Upanishads, the Yogavasishtha, etc.

Daily Discipline of Thoughts

The mind is a mischievous imp. It is like a jumping monkey. It must be disciplined daily. Only then will it gradually come under your control.

It is only by the practical training of your mind that you can prevent bad thoughts and actions from arising and can ward off bad thoughts and actions that have arisen from recurrence.

It is only by practical training of your mind that you can encourage good thoughts and actions to arise, and can sustain good thoughts and actions when they have arisen.

Here is a beautiful daily exercise for mental relaxation. It will pour into you great inspiration and strength. Close the eyes. Think of anything that is pleasant. This will relax the mind in a wonderful manner. Think of the mighty Himalayas, the sacred Ganga, the striking scenery in Kashmir, the Taj Mahal, the Victoria Memorial in Calcutta, a lovely sunset, the vast expanse of ocean or the infinite blue sky.

Imagine that the whole world and your body are floating like a straw in this vast ocean of Spirit. Feel that you are in touch with the Supreme Being. Feel that the life of the whole world is pulsating, vibrating and throbbing through you. Feel that Lord Hiranyagarbha, the ocean of Life, is gently rocking you on His vast bosom. Then open your eyes. You will experience immense mental peace, vigour and strength. Practice this and feel.

Thoughts and the Snake-analogy

Just as fruit is born of the seed, so also deeds are born of thoughts. Good thoughts generate good actions. Evil thoughts produce evil actions.

Harbour good thoughts. Repel evil thoughts. If you cultivate good thoughts by Satsanga, study of religious books, prayer, etc., evil thoughts will die by themselves.

Just as you remove at once the pebble in your shoe that troubles you, so also, you must be able to remove at once any tormenting thought from your mind. Only then have you gained sufficient strength in the control of thought. Only then have you attained some real progress in the spiritual path.

When you give a blow on the head of a snake with a stick and crush its head, it remains absolutely motionless for sometime. You think it is dead. All of a sudden it raises its head and runs away. Even so, the thoughts that were once crushed and suppressed by you regain strength and raise their heads. They must be destroyed totally beyond resurrection.

World-conquest by Thought-conquest

Control the thoughts or Sankalpas. Avoid imagination or day-dreaming. The mind will be annihilated. Extinction of Sankalpas alone is Moksha or release. The mind is destroyed when there is no imagination.

The experience of the world illusion is due to your imagination. It vanishes away when imagination is completely stopped.

Victory over thoughts is really a victory over all limitations, weakness, ignorance and death. The inner war with the mind is more terrible than the outer war with the machine-guns. Conquest of thoughts is more difficult than the conquest of the world by the force of arms. Conquer your thoughts and you would conquer the world.

Form a Divine Channel for Thought-force

Thoughts generally flow with ease towards external objects. The mind can very easily think of worldly objects. It is its Svabhava.

Mental force can easily flow in the old grooves and avenues of mundane thoughts. It finds it extremely difficult to think of God. It is an uphill work for a Samsaric mind of Vyavahara. The difficulty in weaning the mind from worldly thoughts, from external objects, and fixing it on God is the same as in making the Ganga flow towards Gangotri instead of its natural flow towards Ganga-Sagar. It is like rowing against the current of the Yamuna.

Still, through strenuous efforts and Tyaga it must be trained to flow towards God, much against its will, if you want to free yourself from birth and death. There is no other go if you want to escape from worldly miseries and tribulations.

Role of Vigilance in Thought-control

It is very difficult to fix the mind on one thought in the beginning. Diminish the number of thoughts. Try to think of only one subject.

If you think of rose you can have all sorts of thoughts connected with rose only. You can think of different kinds of roses that are grown in different parts of the world. You can think of the various preparations that are made out of roses and their uses. You can allow even thoughts of other kinds of flowers to enter; but do not entertain thoughts of fruits and vegetables.

Check the aimless wandering state of the mind. Do not have thoughts at random when you think of rose. Gradually you can fix the mind on one thought only. You will have to discipline the mind daily. Eternal vigilance is needed in thought-control.

Watch and Spiritualize Your Thoughts

Watch the thoughts. Control the thoughts. Be a witness of your thoughts. Rise above thoughts and dwell in that pure consciousness where there is no thought.

The subtle impressions, tendencies, desires and passions lying in the depths of the subconscious have a tremendous effect on your conscious life. They should be purified and sublimated. They must be given a spiritual turn. Hear what is auspicious. Behold what is auspicious. Think what is auspicious. Talk what is auspicious. Meditate what is auspicious. Understand what is auspicious. Know what is auspicious.

Fear, strong dislike, buried hatred, prejudice, intolerance, anger, lust, disturb the action of the subconscious mind. Cultivate virtues. Purify and strengthen the subconscious mind. Desire, greed, etc., enslave and obscure the mind which must be freed and restored to its pristine purity, to reflect Truth and practice meditation. The lower impulses belong to the physical body and the mental plane.

When the mind does not function owing to the absence of Vasanas (mental impressions and subtle desires), then arises the state of Manonasa or annihilation of the mind.

Chapter 8. The Patterns Of Thought-Culture

Discrimination and Inner Mental Culture

Whenever desires crop in your mind, do not try to fulfil them. Reject them through discrimination, right enquiry and dispassion. You will get tranquillity of mind and mental strength by constant practice. The mind is thinned out. The mind is checked directly from wandering. Its outgoing tendencies are curbed.

If the desires are eradicated, the thoughts also will die by themselves. The mind is detached from the manifold sense-objects by continually observing their defects and is fixed on Brahman.

In the practice of Sama, the five Jnana-Indriyas or organs of knowledge, viz., ear, skin, eye, tongue and nose are also controlled. Sama is serenity of mind produced by the constant eradication of Vasanas or desires.

Unwholesome Thoughts and Self-watchfulness

Fully realize for yourself the grave and ruinous consequences of evil thoughts. This will set you on your guard when the evil thoughts would come. The moment they come, exert yourself or divert the mind to some other object of divine thoughts, prayer or Japa. A real earnestness to drive away the evil thoughts will keep you on the alert so much so that even if they appear in dream you will at once wake up. Should the enemy appear when you are awake, it will not be very difficult for you to cope with him, if only you are sufficiently watchful.

You must be saved from the malformation and the miscarriage of your mind. Mind is like a playful child. The clement energies of the mind must be bent to become the passive channels for the transmission of truth. The mind must be filled with Sattva (purity). It should be trained to think of Truth or God, constantly.

If you want rapid progress in the spiritual path, watch every thought. A vacant mind is ever distressed. It is the devil's workshop. Be thoughtful. Keep guard over your mind. Watch every impulse and thought.

Spiritualize or sublimate your instincts. Evil thought is the most dangerous thief. Slay this thief with the sword of wisdom. Generate daily new divine vibrations or thought-waves in your mind. Make your thought pure, strong, sublime and definite. You will gain immense spiritual strength and peace.

Every thought must be constructive and noble. Thoughts are only refractions. Slay all thoughts. Go thou within to the Light of lights. If you wish to attain Self-realization, imagination and speculation must stop. Purify and control the emotions. Beneath your conscious life, there is a very wide region of subconscious life.

All habits originate from the subconscious plane. Subconscious life is more powerful than your ordinary life of objective consciousness. Through the practice of Yoga you can modify, control and influence the subconscious depths. Take one evil trait. Meditate on its opposite virtue every morning. Practice it during the day. The evil quality will vanish soon. Meditate on mercy in the morning and practice it during the day. You will soon develop mercy.

If evil thoughts enter your mind once in a month instead of thrice weekly (remember that evil thinking is the beginning of adultery), if you become angry once in a month instead of once weekly, that is a sign of progress, that is a sign of your increased will-power; that is a sign of growing spiritual strength. Be of good cheer. Keep a diary of spiritual progress.

Self-development by Yogic Thought-culture

The supraphysical phenomena occurring in the practice of Yoga and the practitioner's experience on subtler planes are viewed with suspicion and regarded as mere oriental magic. Yoga is neither fanciful nor does it contain anything abnormal. It aims at the integral development of all faculties in man. It is the time-tested, rational way to a fuller and more blessed life that will naturally be followed by one and all in the world of tomorrow.

All methods of Yoga have ethical training and moral perfection as their basis. The eradication of vices and the development of certain virtues form the first step in the ladder of Yoga.

The disciplining of your nature and the formation of a steady and pure character through a set of right habits and regular daily observances, is the next step. Upon this firm foundation of a well-established and virtuous moral character is built the further structure of Yoga.

Thought-culture by the Method of Substitution

The substitution method is very easy and effective in the destruction of evil thoughts. Cultivate positive virtuous thoughts of mercy, love, purity, forgiveness, integrity, generosity and humility in the garden of your mind.

The negative vicious thoughts of hatred, lust, anger, greed, pride will die by themselves.

It is difficult to destroy the evil thoughts by attacking them directly. You will have to tax your will and waste your energy.

Spiritual Methods for Thought-culture

If you think again and again of an impure thing it gains new strength. It gets the force of momentum. You must drive it immediately. If you find it difficult to do so, entertain counter-thoughts of God. Cultivate sublime and elevating thoughts. Evil thoughts will die by themselves. A noble thought is a potent antidote to counteract an evil-thought. This is easier than the former method. By repetition of God's Name, thousands of times daily, good thoughts gain new strength. By repeating *'Aham Brahma Asmi'* thousand times daily the idea that you are the spirit (Atman) becomes stronger. The idea that you are the body becomes weaker and weaker.

If evil thoughts enter your mind, don't use your will-force in driving them. You will lose your energy only. You will tax your will only. You will fatigue yourself. The greater the efforts you make, the more the evil thoughts will return with redoubled force. They will return more quickly also. The thoughts will become more powerful. Be indifferent. Keep quiet. They will pass off soon. Or substitute good counter thoughts (Pratipaksha Bhavana method). Or think of the picture of God and the Mantra again and again forcibly. Or pray.

The Importance of Thought-culture

Thought-culture is a vital subject. Very few people know this art or science. Even the so-called educated people are unaware of this fundamental education.

All are victims of random thinking. All sorts of loose thoughts of diverse kinds come and go in the mental factory. There is neither rhythm nor reasoning. There is neither concord nor discipline. All is in a state of utter chaos and confusion. There is no clarification of ideas.

You cannot think of one subject even for two minutes in an orderly and systematic manner. You have no understanding of the laws of thoughts and the laws of the mental plane.

There is a perfect menagerie inside. All sorts of sensual thoughts fight amongst themselves to enter the mind of a sensualist and gain the upper hand. The eye Indriya struggles to bring its own thoughts. It wants to have sight-seeing. The ear Indriya wants to bring only base thoughts, lustful thoughts, thoughts of hatred, jealousy and fear. Many cannot entertain a single, sublime, divine thought even for a second. Their minds are so framed that the mental energy runs in sensual grooves.

The Battle of Thoughts

In the beginning of thought-culture, there is internal fight between pure and impure thoughts. The impure thought tries to enter the mental factory again and again. It asserts: "O little man, you gave me shelter in the beginning. You welcomed me before. You gave me a cordial reception. I have every right to remain in the lowlands of your mind in your instinctive passionate mind. Why are you cruel towards me? I only gave you a push or stimulus in taking you to restaurants and hotels, cinemas and theatres, ball-rooms and bars. You had a variety of enjoyments through me alone. Why are you ungrateful to me now? I will resist, persist and recur again and again. Do whatever you like. You are weak through old habits. You have no strength to resist." Eventually pure thoughts only will gain victory. Sattva is a greater power than Rajas and Tamas. Positive overcomes negative.

Good Thought—The First Perfection

Thought is a good servant. It is an instrument. You will have to utilize it tactfully and properly. The prime requisite for happiness is control over the thoughts.

Your thought is imprinted over your face. Thought is a bridge that connects the human with the Divine. Your body, your business, your home—they are only ideas within your mind. Thought is a dynamic force. Good thought is the first perfection. Thought is real wealth.

Culture the Thoughts and Become a Buddha

Drive away from your mind all unnecessary, useless and obnoxious thoughts. Useless thoughts impede your spiritual growth; obnoxious thoughts are stumbling blocks to spiritual advancement. You are away from God when you entertain useless thoughts. Substitute thoughts of God.

Entertain only thoughts that are helpful and useful. Useful thoughts are stepping-stones to spiritual growth and progress. Do not allow the mind to run into the old grooves and to have its own ways and habits. Be on the careful watch.

You must eradicate through introspection all sorts of mean thoughts, useless thoughts, unworthy thoughts, impure thoughts, all sexual thoughts, thoughts of jealousy, hatred and selfishness. You must annihilate all destructive thoughts of disharmony and discord. You must always develop pure, good, loving, sublime and divine thoughts. Every thought must be of a constructive nature. It must be strong, positive and definite.

The mental image must be of a clear-cut and well-defined thought; it must bring peace and solace to others. It should not bring even the least pain and unhappiness to anyone. Then you are a blessed soul on the earth. You are a mighty power on the earth. You can help many, heal thousands, spiritualize and elevate a large number of persons as did Jesus or Buddha.

Just as you grow jasmine, rose, lily, Honolulu flowers in a garden, so also you should cultivate the flowers of peaceful thoughts of love, mercy, kindness, purity in the vast garden of Antahkarana. Through introspection, you will have to water this garden of mind; with meditation and sublime thinking remove the weeds of vain, useless, discordant thoughts.

Avoid Thoughts of Another Man's Defects

The nature of the mind is such that it becomes that which it intensely thinks of. Thus if you think of the vices and defects of another man, your mind will be charged with these vices and defects at least for the time being.

He who knows this psychological law will never indulge in censuring others or in finding fault in the conduct of others, will see only the good in others, and will always praise others. This practice enables one to grow in concentration, Yoga and spirituality.

Last Thought Determines Next Birth

The last thought of a man governs his future destiny. The last thought of a man determines his future birth. Lord Krishna says in the Bhagavad-Gita, "Whosoever at the end abandoneth the body, thinking upon any being, to that being only he goeth, O Kaunteya, because of his constant thought of that being" (Chapter: VIII-6).

Ajamila lost his pious conduct, and led a detestable living. He fell into evil depth of sinful habits and resorted to theft and robbery. He became a slave of a public woman. He became the father of ten children, the last of whom was called Narayana.

When he was about to die, he was absorbed in the thoughts of his last son. Three fearful messengers of Death advanced towards Ajamila. Ajamila cried aloud in great distress the last son's name 'Narayana'.

On a mere mention of the name of 'Narayana' the attendants of Lord Hari came speedily along and obstructed the messengers of Death. They took him to Vaikuntha or the world of Vishnu.

The soul of Sisupala entered the supreme Lord with an effulgent spark of ineffable glory and magnificence. This vile Sisupala spent his lifetime in reviling Lord Krishna and then he entered the Lord.

The worm on the wall when stung by the wasp changes into the form of the latter. Similarly, the man who focuses his hate on Lord Krishna gets rid of his sins and reaches that Lord by regular devotion as the Gopis did by Kama (passion), Kamsa by fear, Sisupala by hatred and Narada by love.

Lord Krishna says in the Gita, "Whoever constantly thinks of Me intensely and with one-pointed mind, to such steadfast Yogin, I am easily attainable; and having thus reached Me and merged in Me, he is not born again in the fleeting world of woe and misery. O Arjuna! While all the worlds created by Brahma are limited by time and have their moment of dissolution on reaching Me, there is no rebirth, therefore at all times, meditate on Me, the supreme Vaasudeva and with mind and intellect fixed on Me. Doubtless, you will attain Me" (Chapter: VIII-14, 15, 16).

The constant practice of fixing the mind on the Lord, although a man is engaged in worldly pursuits, will enable him to intuitively and automatically think of the Lord, even at the time of his departure. The Lord says: "With the mind thus engaged in the Yoga of constant practice, not deflected by any other obstacles, one attains the supreme Purusha of resplendent glory."

The Lord further says, "At the time of death, he who thinks of My real Being as the supreme Lord Sri Krishna or Narayana, leaves the body and verily reaches My Being. Doubt this not! In whatever form a man thinks of Me at the time of death, that form he attains, that form again being the result of nourishing that thought in a particular groove and by constant meditation of the same."

The Lord further says: "He who further establishes his mind on Me, even at the time of forthgoing and who is in that Divine state of renouncing everything and of dwelling in Brahman or Brahmic state, is free from delusion" (B.G. II-72).

He who has a strong habit of using snuff in his life imitates the act of snuffing with his fingers when he is in an unconscious state just before his death. So strong is the habit of snuffing in this man.

The last thought of a licentious man will be the thought of his woman. The last thought of an inveterate drunkard will be that of his peg of liquor. The last thought of a greedy money-lender will be that of his money. The last thought of a fighting soldier will be that of shooting his enemy. The last thought of a mother who is intensely attached to her only son will be that of her son only.

Raja Bharata nursed a deer out of mercy and became attached to it. His last thought was the thought of that deer. Hence he had to take the birth of a deer, but he had memory of his last birth as he was an advanced soul.

The last thought of a person will be the thought of God only, if that person has disciplined his mind all throughout his life and has tried to fix it on the Lord through constant practice. It cannot come by a practice in a day or two, in a week or a month. It is a life-long endeavour and struggle.

The last thought determines the next birth. The last prominent thought of one's life occupies the mind at the time of death. The predominant idea at the time of death is what in normal life has occupied his attention most. The last thought determines the nature of character of the body to be attained next. As a man thinketh, so shall he become.

The Background of Sattvic Thought

The vast majority of people will always want something concrete to hold on, something around which, as it were, to place their ideas, sometimes which will be the centre of all thought-forms in their minds. That is mind's very nature. A background of thought is needed for fixing the mind.

Have a Sattvic background of thought of mental image. The mind assumes the shape of any object it intensely thinks upon. If it thinks of an orange, it assumes the shape of an orange. If it thinks of Lord Krishna with flute in hand, it assumes the shape of Lord Krishna. You must train the mind properly and give it proper Sattvic food for assimilation.

You must have Sattvic background of thought to take you to the goal (salvation). If you are a devotee of Lord Krishna, have a background of thought of His picture and the repetition of His famous Mantra 'Om Namo Bhagavate Vaasudevaya' and His qualities (Form-formless-qualities). A Nirguna Upasaka (Vedanti) should have a background of thought of 'OM' and its meaning (Infinite Ocean of Light, Satchidananda, Vyapaka, Paripurna-Atman). Work in the world and, the moment the mind is free, begin to think of the background of thought—either Saguna or Nirguna background according to taste, temperament and capacity for Sadhana. By constant thinking, a habit in the mind will be formed and, without effort, the mind will run towards the background of thought.

It is a pity that the vast majority of persons have no ideal, no programme of life at all and no Sattvic background of thought. They are doomed to failure. The background of thought of a young married lady is usually lustful. The background of thought of an old mother is the affection towards her sons and grandsons. The background of thought of the vast majority of persons is hatred and jealousy. Even the so-called educated persons with many university qualifications and academic knowledge which is only husk when compared with spiritual knowledge, have no ideal, no programme of life and no background of thought. A deputy collector, after getting pension, marries a third wife and goes on as a Dewan of a State.

A worldly minded person is a prey to sexual thoughts and thoughts of hatred, anger and revenge. These two types of thoughts actually take possession of his mind. He is a slave to these two sets of thoughts. He does not know how to divert his mind and fix it on some other good, noble thought. He does not know the laws of thought. He is quite unaware of the nature and suitable workings of the mind. His position is extremely deplorable despite his earthly possessions and bookish knowledge obtained in universities. Viveka has not awakened in him. He has no Sraddha in saints, Sastras and God. He is unable to resist an evil desire, craving or temptation on account of his weak will. The only potent remedy to remove his world-intoxication, world-charm, world-delusion is constant Satsanga or association with Sadhus, Sannyasins and Mahatmas.

After retirement, everybody should have a background of thought and should spend his time in philosophical studies and divine contemplation. Old habits of loose thinking must be replaced by cultivating fresh habits of good thoughts. At first, a tendency to think of good thoughts will be formed. By continued practice, a positive, definite habit of thinking of virtuous, helping thoughts will be developed. You will have to struggle very hard.

The old habits will try to recur again and again. Till you are firmly established in the habit of thinking of good thoughts only, you will have to fill the mind again and again with Sattvic thoughts, divine thoughts, thoughts of the Gita, Lord Krishna, Lord Rama, Upanishads, etc. New grooves and avenues will be formed now. Just as a gramophone-needle cuts a small groove in the plate, Sattvic thinking will cut new healthy grooves in the mind and brain. New Samskaras will be formed.

You will have concentration without much effort. He who has subdued his mind beholds in his own Self by the help of his own pure intellect the Immortal, Eternal Brahman which is subtler than the subtlest, which is an embodiment of bliss, peace and wisdom. It is the contact of the sense with the sense-object that gives rise to a mental perception. But if the senses are withdrawn and the mind is stilled there comes a stage where there is no touch with any sense-object.

It is the state of bliss and pure consciousness or Nirvikalpa Samadhi which burns all Samskaras that give rise to birth and death. Attachment is death. You are attached to body, action, wife, children, property, house, place and articles that give you pleasure. Wherever there is attachment there are anger, fear and Vasanas. Attachment leads to bondage. If you want to attain God-realization you must get rid of all sorts of attachment.

The first step in detachment is to be detached from the body with which you feel so much identified. The Sanskrit word for the Self is Atman. Atman is derived from the root '*At*' which means to go always. Atman thus means that which evolves itself always into names and forms of the universe in order to realize His real, essential nature which is Existence-Consciousness-Bliss Absolute.

The Pure Consciousness and Freedom of Thoughts

Through constant and intense practice of Yoga and Jnana Sadhana, you can become waveless, thought-free. The waveless Yogi helps the world more than the man on the platform. Ordinary people can hardly grasp this point. When you are waveless you actually permeate and pervade every atom of the universe, purify and elevate the whole world.

The names of waveless Jnanis such as Jada Bharata and Vamadeva are even now remembered. They never published books. They never made disciples. Yet, what a tremendous influence these waveless Jnanis had produced on the minds of the people!

You can attain Jnana only if you are free from sensuous desires and immoral mental states. Aloofness of body from sensuous objects and aloofness of mind from immoral states of mind are needed for the attainment of Jnana. Then only will Divine Light descend. Just as a bungalow is cleaned of cobwebs and the garden, of all its weeds for the reception of the viceroy, the mental palace should be cleansed of all vices, desires and immoral states for the reception of the Holy Brahman, the Viceroy of viceroys.

When a desire arises in the mind, a worldling welcomes it and tries to fulfil it; but an aspirant renounces it immediately through Viveka. Wise people consider even spark of desire as a very great evil. Therefore they will not entertain any kind of desire. They will be ever delightful in Atman only.

Thinking starts the process of creation. Thinking means externalization or objectification. Thinking means differentiation, quality and multiplicity. Thinking is Samsara. Thinking causes identification with the body. Thinking causes 'I-ness' and 'mine-ness'.

Thinking causes time, space, etc. Stop this thinking through Vairagya and Abhyasa, and merge yourself in the Pure Consciousness. Where there is no thinking or Sankalpa, there is Absolution or Jivanmukti.

Chapter 9. From Thoughts To Thought-Transcendence

Thoughts and Life

Man thinks of sensual objects and gets attached to them. He thinks that fruits are very good for the body. He exerts to possess them. Then he actually possesses and enjoys them. He now clings to the fruits. He develops a habit of taking fruits now and when he fails to obtain them any day, he gets pain.

From thinking comes attachment; from attachment desire is born; from desire proceeds anger, anger arises when desire is frustrated by some cause or the other; from anger arises delusion; from delusion, failure of memory; from failure of memory, loss of intellect; from loss of intellect man is totally ruined. If you want to attain everlasting peace, do not think of objects, but think always of the immortal blissful Atman alone.

Desires by themselves are harmless. They are galvanized by the power of thought. Then only they do much havoc. Man muses or thinks on the objects of the senses. He imagines that he will get a great deal of pleasure from them. This imagination excites the desires. This power of imagination co-operates with the desires. Then the desires are invigorated or vitalized. They attack the deluded Jiva vehemently.

Thoughts and Character

Man is not a creature of circumstances. His thoughts are the architects of his circumstances. A man of character builds a life out of circumstances. He steadily perseveres and plods. He does not look back. He marches forward bravely.

He is not afraid of obstacles. He never frets and fumes. He never gets discouraged and disappointed. He is full of vigour, energy, vim and vitality. He is ever zealous and enthusiastic.

Thoughts are the bricks with which character is built. Character is not born. It is formed. Determination to build definite character in life is needed. This must be followed up with persistent striving.

Build your character; you can shape your life. Character is power; it is influence; it makes friends. It draws patronage and support. It creates friends and funds. It opens a sure and easy way to wealth, honour, success and happiness.

Character is the determining factor in victory and defeat, success and failure, and in all the issues of life. A man of good character enjoys life herein and hereafter.

Small kind acts, small courtesies, small consideration, small benevolence, habitually practiced in your social intercourse give a great charm to your character than great platform lectures, discourses, oration, exhibition of talents, etc.

Strong character is formed by strong and noble thinking. A good character is the fruition of personal exertion. It is the result of one's own endeavours.

It is not wealth or power nor is it mere intellect that governs the world. It is moral character associated with moral excellence that really rules the entire universe.

Nothing in this world—wealth, name, fame, victory—is worth a fig or a straw, without character. Character must stand behind and back up everything. And, character is built by your thoughts.

Thoughts and Words

There is power in every word that is spoken. There are two kinds of Vrittis or thoughts, viz., Sakti Vritti and Lakshana Vritti in words.

In the Upanishads, the Lakshana Vritti is taken. 'Vedasvarupoham' does not mean 'Embodiment of Vedas.' The Lakshana Vritti does denote 'Brahman' who can be reached by the study of the Upanishads alone: by the Sabda-Pramana alone.

Mark here the power in the words. If anyone calls another 'Sala' or 'Badmash' or 'fool', he is thrown into a state of fury immediately. Fight ensues. If you address anyone as 'Bhagavan' or 'Prabhu' or 'Maharaj', he is immensely pleased.

Thoughts and Actions

Thoughts are dormant seeds of action. The mind's acts, and not the bodily acts, are alone true acts. It is the actions of the mind that are truly termed Karmas.

Thought and act are interdependent. There is no such thing as mind apart from thought. Thoughts constitute the mind.

Words are nothing but the outward expressions of thoughts which are imperceptible. Actions are caused by feelings of desire and aversion (likes and dislikes). These feelings are caused by the fact that you attribute a pleasurable or painful nature to objects. Thought is finite. It is inadequate to express even temporal processes, not to speak of the absolute which is inexpressible. The body with its organs is no other than the mind.

Thoughts, Peace and Strength

Fewer the desires, lesser the thoughts. Become absolutely desireless. The wheel of mind will stop entirely. If you reduce your wants, if you do not try to fulfil your desires, if you try to eradicate your desires one by one, your thoughts will diminish in frequency and length. The number of thoughts also per minute will diminish.

Fewer the thoughts, greater the peace. Remember this always. A wealthy man who is engaged in speculation in a big city and who has a large number of thoughts has a restless mind in spite of his comforts, whereas a Sadhu who lives in the cave of the Himalayas and who is practicing thought-control is very happy in spite of his poverty.

Fewer the thoughts, greater the mental strength and concentration. Suppose that the average number of thoughts that pass through your brain within one hour is one hundred. If you succeed in reducing it, by constant practice of concentration and meditation, to ninety, you have gained ten per cent of the power of concentration of mind.

Every thought that is reduced adds strength and peace to the mind. Reduction of even one thought will give mental strength and peace of mind. You may not be able to feel this in the beginning as you do not possess a subtle intellect, but there is a spiritual thermometer inside to register the reduction of even a single thought. If you reduce one thought, the mental strength that you have gained by this reduction will help you to reduce the second thought easily.

Thought, Energy and Sacred Thoughts

Thought is a finer manifestation of being than ether or energy. You think, because you share the universal thought.

Thought is both force and motion. Thought is dynamic. Thought moves. Thought decides the future. As you think, so you become. Thought makes a saint or a sinner. Thought can shape a man. Think that you are Brahman and Brahman you become.

Sacred thoughts generate and sustain divine thoughts. Thoughts of hatred interfere with the inner harmony of the heart. Every useless thought is wastage of energy. Useless thoughts are obstacles to spiritual growth. Every thought must have a definite purpose.

Negative evil thoughts cannot overcome fear. Patience overcomes anger and irritability. Love overcomes hatred. Purity overcomes lust. Mind is not daily made; in every minute it changes its colour and shape.

Thoughts That Bind

Through its power of differentiation, mind generates this universe. The expansion of the mind's thoughts towards sensual objects is bondage.

The abandoning of the thoughts constitutes liberation. The mind creates, at the outset, an attachment for the body and sense-objects and binds the man through this attachment. The attachment is due to the force of Rajas.

Sattva brings non-attachment and infuses in the mind discrimination and renunciation.

It is the Rajasic mind that causes the ideas 'I' and 'mine' and the difference of body, caste, creed, colour, order of life, etc.

The poisonous tree of the Mayaic illusion grows more and more out of the seed of the mind's modification or expanded thoughts in the soil of the multifarious enjoyments of the world.

From Pure Thoughts to Transcendental Experience

Thoughts are of two kinds: pure thoughts and impure thoughts. Desire to do virtuous actions, Japa, meditation, study of religious books, etc., is pure thought. A desire to go to cinema, to hurt others and to seek sex-relations, is impure thought.

Impure thoughts should be destroyed by the increase of pure thoughts, and pure thoughts also should be given up in the end.

Thoughts gain strength by repetition of sensual enjoyments. Sensual enjoyments leave on the mind, subtle impressions.

The real Svarupa of mind is Sattva only. Rajas and Tamas join Sattva accidentally in the middle. They can be removed by Sadhana or purificatory practices such as Tapas, selfless service, Dama, Sama, Japa, worship, etc. If you develop the Daivi Sampat or divine qualities, Rajas and Tamas will perish. Then the mind will be pure, subtle, steady and one-pointed. Then it will melt in the subtle invisible homogeneous Brahman (Akhandaikarasa Brahman). It will mix with Brahman now, just as milk mixed with milk, water with water, oil with oil. Nirvikalpa Samadhi will result.

Raja Yogic Method for Thought-transcendence

Substitute pure thoughts for impure thoughts. This method of substitution will destroy all evil thoughts. This is very easy. This is the method of Raja Yoga.

The method of driving the thoughts at once by will-force or by using the formula "get out, O evil thoughts" is very taxing. It is not suitable for ordinary people. It demands tremendous will-power and spiritual strength.

You must rise above pure thoughts and attain the supreme state of thoughtlessness. Only then can you rest in your own Svarupa. Only then will Brahman be revealed like Amalaka fruit in the palm of your hand.

Vedantic Technique for Thought-transcendence

When all kinds of useless thoughts and emotions trouble you much, be indifferent (Udasina). Say to yourself: "Who am I?" Feel: "I am not the mind. I am the Atman, the all-pervading Spirit, Suddha Satchidananda. How can emotions affect me? I am Nirlipta, unattached; I am Sakshi, witness of these emotions. Nothing can disturb me." When you repeat these suggestions of Vichara or Vedantic reflection, the thoughts and emotions will die by themselves.

This is the Jnana-method of driving out thoughts and emotions and the struggling with the mind.

When any thought arises in the mind, enquire: Why has this Vritti (modification) arisen? Whom it concerns? Who am I? All the thoughts will die eventually. All mental activities will cease. The mind will turn inward. It will rest in Atman. This is Vedantic Sadhana. You will have to persist constantly in the Sadhana.

Whatever stray thoughts arise, the one thought 'Who am I' will destroy all other thoughts of worldly nature. That thought will die by itself. Ego will vanish. Balance left is Kevala Asti; Chinmatra; Kevala Suddha Chaitanya; Chidakasamatra which is Nama-rupa-rahita (free from all names and forms), Vyavahara-rahita, Malavasana-rahita, Nishkriya, Niravayava, which is Santa-Siva-Advaita of the Mandukya Upanishad. That is Atman. That is to be known.

Chapter 10. The Metaphysics Of Thought Power

Thought Power and Practical Idealism—1

Man goes from bad to worse in the scale of life. He does not put his total strength in fit action; so he does not have the richest return of wisdom. Man is tormented by imperfections. Grudges are foaming in his mind because his life is not flowing with right energy. The love of 'me' is ever ready to accuse the other party. Objects of the objective world are delicious torments for him. Still the man wants to stand on the firm basis of personal feelings. Torn by his personal passions, he is unable to establish proper and harmonious relations with others. He is always seeking his private felicity in every circumstance.

Altar of truth demands the oblations of mental rigidity, harshness, self-assertion, eccentricity and egoism. Train yourself for that truth which knows no partiality, no sex, no wandering gleam, O man. There is stain of error in daily experiences of man. That is why his life is defaced and disfigured. Men have become vinegar for each other's eyes by their wrong thoughts.

The ice of ill-will is chilling their heart. Men are bound to each other by every sort of tie, by blood, by pride, by fear, by hope, by lucre, by lust, by hate, by admiration, by every circumstance, but not by spiritual love. This is all due to wrong thoughts.

The wise man makes an island which no flood can overwhelm. The scent of flowers does not travel against the wind, but the odour of a wise man travels against the wind; he pervades every place by his thoughts. He is like a snowy mountain which can be seen from afar.

O man! If you fill your lamp with water you will not be able to dispel the darkness. Feed your lamp with the oil of right thoughts. Let the right views become the torch to light your way. Do not seek to gratify your vanity and self-seeking pride.

On the brink of truth man is miserably dying. All evil thoughts are embodied in bad physiognomies. But there is nothing to despair, because there is never darkness without light. There is always a sublime answer to every human need. All things are possible to those who believe in the possibility.

O man! Raise your sight to right direction and use right laws. Set in motion positive thoughts.

Remember your objective. It is easy to be diverted into an excursion into side-tracks.

A holy thought is a voice. It speaks when the tongue is silent. It struggles and comes out of all obstructions serenely and no power on the earth can suppress it for a long period. O man! Do not trade in unrealities.

Do not try to embrace happiness in a thousand ways. The faster you will follow it the swifter it will fly from you. Do not become a thorn for yourself as well as for others.

Change the direction of your thoughts. Scrutinize your thoughts. Where necessity ends, curiosity begins. No sooner you are supplied with everything, than you sit down and entertain the thoughts of artificial appetites. That is why you have crossed the boundary of law.

By your own thoughts you make or mar your world. Inevitable law of reaction is such, O man! that whatever you will harbour in the inmost chamber of your heart, will shape itself in your outward life. Chance seems to form the surface of reality, but deep down, thought-forces are at work. Nothing in this universe and in daily behaviour is merely accidental. So improve your thoughts.

Real action is in silent moments. Purified thought revives the entire manner of life; it tells the man quietly "you have done thus but it were better done some other way."

The thoughts you entertain during the time of reflection, let them not become inaudible when you are engrossed in daily duties. Arm yourself with the sublime thoughts.

By no other way does one come directly to the knowledge of truth, than through one's own thinking and experience. Divine thought reduces centuries and makes itself present through all ages. Entertain divine thoughts.

Thought Power and Practical Idealism—2

Wash off the baser thoughts with the help of higher thoughts and when the washing is effected, cling to neither of them. The present state of your experience is due to the thinking, feeling and acting of incalculable past lives. It cannot be easily got rid of without prolonged process of thinking of and practice.

Thought is ancestor of action. If you want to improve your actions purify your thoughts.

Become a staunch believer in self-reliance and self-effort. You can determine your fate by force of thoughts. As clouds are the main source of rain, so the control of one's own thoughts is the source of durable prosperity. You are yourself your own friend or enemy. If you will not save yourself by cherishing good thoughts, there is no other remedy.

Mind is the only creator. Everything is created through the mind. It is absolutely free in creating a world for itself. Whenever the mind is referred to as the creator of external objects, it must be considered as the cosmic mind and a part of Isvara Srishti.

Whenever the mind is referred to in relation to psychological functions such as love and hatred, etc., it must be considered as the individual mind and as a part of Jiva Srishti. O man! The real God lives in your heart and the only way to worship the real God residing within the temple of your body is by your own sublime thoughts. Stop the psychological functions of your mind and see value only in sublime thoughts.

The nature of things around you is as you think it to be. Your life is what you make it by your thoughts. Thoughts are the bricks by which you have built the building of your personality. Thought determines destiny. The world around you is the reflex of your thoughts.

You experience as you think. Your own imagination plays havoc with you. You have made yourself timid by entertaining the thoughts of fear. Do not become liberal in imagination.

You are affected by things only in accordance with your idea about them. The mind sees value only in that in which it has intense faith. Though all of you see the same object, everyone of you attach to it different values. According to your mental propensities you think.

Thought is a creative instrument, and man becomes what he thinks upon. Character is thought-formed. You are born with what you have thought upon, and your present character is an index of your previous thoughts. You create your future by your thoughts now; if you think nobly, you will be noble in conduct. If you think basely no environment will make you different. Thus, thoughts and actions are interdependent. Be vigilant and allow only good thoughts in your mental field.

Every one of you have a different conception of duty, value, enjoyment and liberation in accordance with your different convictions. You strive after your own ideal.

You work in accordance with your long-standing and intensified thought and belief. You accomplish and achieve the object of your own desire. Do not let your mind become denser and denser by allowing it to be engrossed in gross forms. Follow the abstractive process by cherishing the thoughts of virtue.

Your present life has three aspects, physical, mental and spiritual. You are tenaciously attached to the physical aspect. Be above physical sensations and other appetites by cherishing the thoughts that you are not body alone, that you are residing in the temple of a body for a short period only. Be above mental titillations. Subjective action functions in the world of thought.

Send out a steady stream of thought and good-will to all creation. The energising motive behind every thought should be service and friendliness.

You are sensible of knack, skill and tricks, but there is an overpowering law which confutes your tricky thoughts and talents. So do not try to become partial half-light. This law constrains everyone to pass for what he is. His thoughts speak from his character and not from his tongue. Do not try to put on an artificial personality. Be genuine and clean in your thoughts.

The stream of thought flows in both directions. When it is flowing towards good, it makes for freedom and knowledge. When it is flowing towards the whirlpool of existence, downward towards non-discrimination, it is then flowing towards evil. The thinking faculty, reaches its summit in light, when it acts according to ethical rules.

You are the centre of individual willing, individual thinking, and individual feeling. The enchantment of time and place presents before you heavenly scenes which vanish like optical illusions. You have repeatedly allowed yourself to be mocked by them; that is why your chest is sawed by the friction of sighs, your discriminative power is dried up by the fire of knowledge. The spiritual goal is held before you. How quickly or how slowly you move towards it, will depend on your thoughts.

Stand united with your higher thoughts. You will achieve that goal which is bought by many failures. Become a non-seeker of personal ends and glory. Death will not easily come near you, if you will not wear on your bosom the necklace of vicious thoughts.

The bliss that accrues from the culture of mind surpasses even the prosperity of the three worlds, or possession of all kinds of jewels, or acquisition of high office.

Your mind is omnipotent. It is capable of accomplishing everything. As you imagine within your mind, so things happen forthwith. Whatever is intensely thought by your mind, that comes to be materialized and effected.

Your thought is endowed with creative power. It can evolve objects from within itself. It is the only creator. Nothing ever will be created or recreated except through mind. Thought is the material out of which things are made. All matter is but materialization of consciousness.

No other being is responsible for what you acquire, as everything is the consequence of your thought. The cause of whatever comes to you in life, is within you. No other agency can bestow favours on you, unless you deserve them. Whatever you get through others, is the outcome of your own thoughts and efforts. There is nothing in the world which you cannot achieve, when your thoughts are flowing in the right direction. You should neither become a pessimist nor a misanthrope.

Creative power is the privilege of every mind. Your own efforts guided by your aspiration are the warp and woof of your destiny. Do not possess a dissipated mind by cherishing weak thoughts. Superficial mind cannot acquire depth of insight.

Control the roving mind by entertaining one flow of thought. All that is intensely thought by you, will come to you early or late, in accordance with the effort you have put in to acquire it.

The extent of space as well as the duration of time are relative to your thoughts and emotions. You experience as you think. If a moment is imagined to be a long period, it is experienced as such and vice versa. The same period of time is experienced as a long age when you are in trouble, and as a moment when you are happy.

Such is the power of thought that sweet is experienced as bitter and vice versa by intense thought. You can turn poison into nectar. Think of Mira. She turned poison into nectar by her intensified thoughts.

You are surrounded by the forces of antagonism. But if there are no thoughts of antagonism in you, you can easily return a blessing for a curse. Thus you can control all the forces of antagonism. Struggle hard and check the unwanted mental rush.

The world around you is only what you believe it to be. Your perceptions are coloured by your thoughts. Your mind perceives and continues to perceive the things in that very form in which it imagines it to be with full faith. Pierce through the steel-armour of biased thoughts, and try to see the divinity in every object.

It is by thought alone that you get into delusion, undergo the experience of birth and death, are bound in the world and become released from it.

All your states of happiness or misery in heaven or hell, are effects of your own thoughts. Early or late, in this life or lives to come, all your passing thoughts will be realized. So, discriminate nicely.

Your present state has been willed by your thoughts. You can change the present state into another by your own thoughts. If you believe that you are separate from the Absolute, you are so. If you think yourself to be Brahman you are so. You limit yourself by your thoughts.

With each divine thought, the mind rends the thin rinds of the visible and finite and comes out into eternity, but you are so negligent about your mental factory.

Thought Power and Practical Idealism—3

Your destiny is mapped out by your thoughts. You have only that much power as you imagine you have. The world around you is as you have willed it to be.

You are living in an infinite ocean of power and cheerfulness, but you appropriate only so much from it as you think, believe and imagine. Due to certain propensities you cherish certain thoughts, and you allow your mind to foment. But by discrimination, you can easily give up the phantasy of mind.

The limit of your thought is the limit of your possibilities. Your circumstances and environments are the materialization of your thoughts. The world experience rises or falls in accordance with your thoughts. Whatever thought is cherished by you in the world will be ultimately realized.

Whatever a pure mind strongly believes something to be, that it soon becomes. Your thoughts are powerful in proportion to your intensity, depth, and warmth. They become so when they are being constantly cherished over and over again. Constant thinking, desiring or imagining of the same idea contributes much to the materialization of that idea.

Develop a pure mind and whatever objects and worlds you wish to get, you will gain those objects and worlds.

It is true that every thought you think has its corresponding effect on the whole or some part of human anatomy. The physical body is realized to be subtle by means of constant meditation on its being so. The mental or subtle body becomes physical when it is repeatedly imagined. The secret of success is constant and repeated effort.

Develop strong determination. It is an important factor which will contribute to the realization of your thoughts. There is nobody who will be able to withstand the power of your determined mind. You can realize everything.

Your body is your objectified thought. When your thoughts change, the body will also change. The mind creates the body from the material of your own thoughts. Thought is a force that can change, transform, or at least modify, almost anything in the human system.

The disorder and disharmony of the physical body is called a physical disease and the conflict of the mind is called a mental disease. Both of them have their ultimate root in ignorance and can be cured only by the knowledge of reality. When you worry about the experiences of the world, a depressing mental disturbance originates in your mind. By the effect of mental disturbance, the smooth and regular flow of vital currents is disturbed. When the vital currents flow improperly, the Nadis become disorganized. Some of them get more vital energy and some get less. Thus, the whole system becomes out of order. In this way mental disharmony is the cause of physical diseases, which can be cured only by removing the cause.

Every depressing and disturbing thought that enters your brain, has a depressing effect on every cell of your body, and tends to produce disease. All negative thoughts are forerunners of disease, and they are messengers of death.

If you want to live long and lead a sensible and healthy life cherish good thoughts. Subtle and powerful are influences of the thoughts in building and rebuilding of your body. Be vigilant.

Practically all diseases with their sufferings have their origin in perverted mental and emotional states and conditions. Restoration of mental harmony is absolutely necessary for you. Purify your thoughts by performing noble actions and by association with wise ones. When your thoughts are purified the vital currents will begin to flow properly and will clean the whole system.

Every good thought stimulates the heart, improves the digestive system and promotes the normal action of every gland.

Contentment is another name for the harmony of the mind. When your thoughts do not wander to this or that object and when you feel self-satisfied, you are in a state of joy which is unique. If you are happy within, everything appears good and pleasing to you.

Thoughts are the main source of your cheerfulness. Purify your thoughts; all troubles will be cured.

If you are cherishing peaceful thoughts the whole world will appear cool, but if negative thoughts have spread their kingdom then the world will seem to be a hot furnace. No circumstance compels you to cherish evil thoughts. Do not ruin yourself by your imagination of fate. It has no reality of its own.

Thought is able to reveal reality. Propelled by right thoughts the wise man is able to come out of most dangerous situations. The whole reality is present in its full potency everywhere, so whatever is intensely thought of anywhere can be experienced there. The essential nature of all objects is thoughts. Materiality is a wrong idea. As snow melts in water through heat, so mind becomes subtle through the practice of right vision and positive thoughts.

The real action is thought only. It is really mental and not physical. The physical action is only an external expression of the real action which is vibration of volition in the mind. Your physical activities are only the various sides of mental activities.

As the beauty of a tree increases immensely in the spring season, so also your strength, your intellect and the lustre will increase in proportion to your positive thoughts. Thoughts of the wise men are entirely different from the thoughts of ordinary people. You are liberated in proportion to your thoughts of indifference to the world.

When thoughts of purity emanate around you, Eternal Law begins to support you. You are aware of your thoughts. You only know what has come to pass in your own experience. In everyone of you separately has arisen the world of the experience of the world. You have got a limited mind which is subject to various types of modes and circumstances.

Some Thought-seeds

True knowledge is spiritual consciousness. It is awareness of one's real nature. Knowledge means right discernment or correct evaluation, wisdom and a perfect understanding of oneself and of others. Right thought results in right action and right life.

Beauty is essentially spiritual. Real beauty lies in one's heart. It is in one's character. Beauty dwells in purity. Beauty shines in virtues. Love is a refined, innate sense of oneness with the entire creation. Love is self-denial, selflessness. Love is sacredness of heart. Love is unrestrained goodwill, mercy, compassion and tolerance. Love is absence of sensuality.

The body is not everything. There is something which is vitally important, which dwells in the body. It is the spirit of man. Though identical with the cosmic Spirit, it is individualized by the Karmas of the individual soul. The body passes away; the spirit lives. The individuality of the spirit is there as long as the body lasts; then it ought to return back to and dissolve itself in its original source, unless of course, it is drawn back by its associated Karmas into another embodiment in order to reap them.

Everything passeth away. Nothing ever is to accompany man except his Karmas, when the body is cast off. Hence as long as man lives, he should live amicably, with love and goodwill towards all, hurting no one in any manner, coveting no worldly riches, with more of kindness and mental charity, forgiveness and tolerance, with detachment to mundane objects, and dissociation of the ego from one's actions, while taking care to acquire no new Karmas as one works out the already accomplished ones.

With a little of contentment, discrimination, devotion to God and self-surrender to His Will, with a little of detachment and non-expectation of anything from anyone, with an attitude of prayerfulness and abiding by the dictates of one's conscience with unshakable faith in one's spiritual principles and code of conduct, and evaluation, life becomes easier, worthier and happier. If you have difficulties, you should look to the cause first. The real trouble lies in ignoring the cause. If the cause is remedied, difficulties become less, or rather accidental. The world is a great school where people are given ample opportunities to mend and mould themselves into better individuals.

No one is born perfect. There are possibilities for everyone to improve oneself. Trials and difficulties ought to make one a better individual rather than create complexes and constrict the mind and heart. Take shelter in great and noble thoughts, and obtain perfection.

Guru's grace is always with the disciple, unreserved and unconditioned. It depends, however, on the self-discipline, faith and purity of the disciple whether to make use of this grace or not. Guru resides in the hearts of his disciples. Some are aware of this and some are not. The living presence of the Guru within is the best asset of the disciple.

Chapter 11. Thought Power For God-Realization

Life—An Interplay of Thoughts

The thought that you hold, will manifest in your life. If you are courageous, cheerful, compassionate, tolerant and kind then these qualities will manifest in your physical life. The only impurity of the mind is base thought and desire.

Guard your good thoughts as an alert watchman guards the treasury. When there is not the 'I'-thought then there will be no other thought.

Life is an interplay of thoughts. Duality ceases when the mind stops its function. Thinking is bound by the time-factor. Thinking must cease. Then alone you will attain the Timeless. Be still.

Let all the waves of thought subside. In that stillness, when the mind melts, there shines the self-effulgent Atman, the pure Consciousness. Watch the mind. Watch the thoughts. Pursue serenity. Make your heart a fitting abode for the Lord.

Thought Results in Spiritual Experience

The molten gold, which is poured into a crucible assumes the shape of the crucible. Even so, the mind assumes the form of the object which it pervades.

The mind assumes the shape of any object it intensely thinks upon. If it thinks of an orange, it assumes the shape of an orange.

If it thinks of Lord Krishna, it assumes the form of Lord Krishna. You must train the mind properly, and give it proper Sattvic food for assimilation. Have a Sattvic background of thought or mental image.

The same thoughts which are entertained by the man during the day, occupy his mind during dream also. If you have purity and concentration, you can make the mind assume any Bhava you like. If you think of mercy, your whole being will be saturated with mercy. If you think of peace, the whole being will be pervaded with peace.

It is the mental Bhava or attitude that determines the nature of an action and brings its fruits. You may embrace your mother or sister or your wife. The action is the same but the mental Bhava is different.

Watch your Bhavana, ideas and feelings always. Your Bhavana should always be Sattvic. You should always entertain Brahma-Bhavana. Watch the Bhavana during the meditation. You need not watch the breath.

The thoughts you create in your mind and the images you form in your daily life will help you in making what you are or what you want to become. If you constantly think of Lord Krishna, you will become identical with the Lord. You will abide in Him for ever.

Thoughts of God

Your mind must be empty of all worldly thoughts. It must be filled with thoughts of God and with nothing else.

Keep your mind filled with good, divine, sublime lofty thoughts, so that there will be no room for evil thoughts. Never speak any unnecessary word. Never allow any unnecessary or vain thought to occupy your mind.

Divine Thoughts for Freedom from Diseases

The best medicine or panacea for all diseases and for keeping good health, is the entertaining of divine thoughts. The waves released by divine thoughts, by Kirtan, Japa and regular meditation, will electrify, rejuvenate, vivify, energise the cells, tissues, nerves.

Another cheap and potent drug is to keep oneself always joyful and cheerful. Study Gita daily, one or two chapters with meaning. Keep yourself fully occupied which is a remedy to keep off thoughts of worldliness.

Fill the mind with Sattva and enjoy wonderful health and peace. Obtain an association with the wise, cultivate faith, serenity, truthfulness, courage, mercy, devotion, love, cheerfulness, confidence, divine thought and divine virtues.

Allow the mind to run in the spiritual direction, in divine grooves; your mind will be peaceful and generate harmonious vibrations. You will enjoy excellent mental health and have no physical disease.

Thought-culture by Knowledge and Devotion

Sit in a solitary place and watch your thoughts carefully. Allow the monkey mind to jump in its own way for some time. After some time it will climb down. It will become quiet. Be a Sakshi or witness of the menagerie of various thoughts in the eternal circus or show. Become a spectator of the mental bioscopic film.

Do not identify with the thoughts. Take an indifferent attitude. All thoughts will die by themselves one by one.

Repeat mentally, "Om I am Sakshi. Who am I? I am thoughtless Atman. I have nothing to do with these false mental pictures and thoughts. Let them roll on. I have no concern with them." All thoughts will perish. The mind will perish like the gheeless lamp.

Fix the mind on the form of Lord Hari or Lord Siva or Lord Krishna or your Guru or any saint like Lord Buddha or Lord Jesus. Again and again try to call this mental image of the picture. All thoughts will die. This is another method, the method of Bhaktas.

Thoughts and Yoga Practice of Mental Quietude

Sit peacefully. Discriminate. Dissociate yourself from thoughts and the mind which is the thinking principle or entity.

Identify yourself with the innermost Self and stand as a silent witness or Sakshi. Gradually all thoughts will die by themselves. You will become one with the supreme Self or Para Brahman.

Continue the practice of mental quietude. It does require, doubtless a direct effort to annihilate the mind.

You should annihilate the Vasanas first. Then alone you will be able to do the Sadhana of mental quiet vigorously. Without producing Vasana-Kshaya, no mental quiet or annihilation of the mind is possible.

Winning Friends by Practice of Yoga

"Win friends and influence people": This Dale Carnagie principle is but a leaf out of the ancient Indian volume on psycho-spiritual science. Practice Yoga; the entire world will worship you. You will unconsciously attract to yourself every living being; even gods will be at your beck and call. Even among wild beasts and bloody brutes you will "win friends." Serve all; love all. Unfold your inner powers through the practice of Raja Yoga, through the control and conquest of thought power.

Through the practice of Yoga, you can make the whole humanity and all living beings members of your own family. Through the practice of Yoga you can overcome all difficulties and can eradicate all weaknesses.

Through the practice of Yoga pain can be transmuted into bliss, death into immortality, sorrow into joy, failure into success and sickness into perfect health. Therefore, practice Yoga diligently.

The Yogic State of Thoughtlessness

Generally there is no genuine spiritual awakening in students. There is mere curiosity for getting some psychic or Yogic powers. That student is far from God as long as he retains some hidden desires for Siddhis. Strictly observe the ethical rules.

Transform the worldly nature first. If you become absolutely desireless, absolutely thoughtless, absolutely Vrittiless, if the mental Vrittis are destroyed in toto, Kundalini will ascend by itself, without effort, through the force of purity. Remove the dross of mind. You will yourself get help and answer from within.

Yogi of the Developed Thought Power

The Yogi who has developed his powers of thoughts, has a magnetic and charming personality. Those who come in contact with him are much influenced by his sweet voice, powerful speech, lustrous eyes, brilliant complexion, strong healthy body, good behaviour, virtuous qualities and Divine Nature.

People derive joy, peace and strength from him. They are inspired by his speech and get elevation of mind by mere contact with him.

Thought moves. Thought is a great force. A Yogi or sage can purify the whole world with his powerful thoughts though he remains in a solitary cave in the Himalayas.

It is not necessary that he should appear on the platform and deliver lectures and discourses to help the people. Sattva is intense activity. The wheel that revolves very rapidly appears to be at rest. So is Sattva. So is a Sattvic man.

Thought-boats to Infinite Strength

Life is a journey from impurity to purity, from hatred to cosmic love, from death to immortality, from imperfection to perfection, from slavery to freedom, from diversity to unity, from ignorance to eternal wisdom, from pain to eternal bliss, from weakness to infinite strength.

Let every thought take you nearer the Lord, every thought further your evolution.

Chapter 12. Thought Power For A New Civilization

Pure Thoughts—Their Impact on the World

The western psychologists and occultists lay great emphasis and stress on the purity of thoughts. Thought-culture is an exact science. One should cultivate right thinking and should drive out all sorts of vain and worldly thoughts.

He who entertains evil thoughts causes great harm unto himself and to the world at large. He pollutes the thought-world. His evil thoughts enter the minds of others who live at a long distance, because thought moves with a tremendous lightning speed.

Evil thoughts are the direct cause for all sorts of diseases. All diseases take their origin at first from an impure thought. He who entertains good, sublime and divine thoughts does immense good unto himself and to the world also. He can radiate joy, hope, solace and peace to his friends who live at a distance.

Thought Power for World-weal

Karma is action and also the law of cause and effect. All kingdoms below the human kingdom are 'mindless'. Therefore they cannot generate thoughts. Further they have no idea of right and wrong, what ought to be done and what ought not to be done and so they cannot create Karma.

Thoughts are solid things, more solid than a lump of sugar-candy. They have tremendous force or power. Utilize this thought power carefully. It can serve you nicely in a variety of ways. But do not misuse this power at random. If you misuse this power, you will have quick downfall or a terrible reaction. Utilize it to help others.

Thought Power for Cultivation of Courage and Love

Destroy ruthlessly the fear-thoughts, selfish thoughts, the hate-thoughts, lustful thoughts, and other morbid negative thoughts. These evil thoughts induce weakness, disease, disharmony, depression and despair.

Cultivate positive thoughts such as mercy, courage, love and purity. The negative thoughts will die by themselves. Try this and feel your strength. Pure thoughts will infuse in you a new exalted life.

Sublime divine thoughts produce tremendous influence in the mind and drive away evil thoughts and change the mental substance. Mind is wholly changed into light by entertaining divine thoughts.

Thought Power for an Ideal Life

Entertain loftiest thoughts. Your character will be exalted. Your life will be noble and ideal.

But, different people have different mental backgrounds. People vary in their capacities, mental and intellectual, and in physical and mental strength to do things. Therefore each of you should have an ideal which is suited to your temperament, your capacity, and realize it with great enthusiasm and dynamic action.

The ideal of one person will not suit another. If one keeps an ideal that he cannot realize, an ideal that is beyond his reach and capacity, he will get disappointment. He will give up his effort and become Tamasic.

You should have your own ideal. You may realize it this moment or after ten years with faltering steps. It does not matter much. Everyone should endeavour his or her level best to live upto this ideal. Your whole energy, nerve-force and will must be put in the realization of the ideal.

You can chalk out your own ideal yourself according to your own standard. If you are unable to do this, have your guide and he will select for you the ideal that is suitable to your capacity and standard.

One should not treat a man, who has a low ideal, with contempt. He may be a baby-soul, who is just crawling now in his moral or spiritual path. Your duty is to help him in all possible ways in the realization or accomplishment of his ideal. You should give him all sorts of encouragement in his sincere endeavour to live up to his own highest ideal.

It is highly deplorable to note that the vast majority of persons have no ideal at all. Even educated persons do not cherish any ideal. They lead an aimless life and therefore are drifted hither and thither like a piece of straw.

They make no progress in life. Is this not a very sad plight? Highly lamentable indeed! It is very difficult to get a human birth and yet people do not realize the importance of keeping up an ideal and living up to the ideal.

The idea of "Eat, drink and be merry," is adopted by the Epicureans, the gluttons and rich people. This school of thoughts has countless followers and the number is increasing by leaps and bounds daily.

This is the ideal of Virochana. This is the ideal of Asuras and Rakshasas. This ideal will lead a man to the dark region of misery and sorrow.

Blessed is the man who elevates his thoughts, keeps up an ideal and struggles hard to live up to his own ideal, for he will soon attain God-consciousness.

Thought-energy for Service and Spiritual Progress

Even as energy is wasted in idle talk and gossiping, so also energy is wasted in entertaining useless thoughts.

Therefore, you should not waste even a single thought. Do not waste even an iota of energy in useless thinking.

Conserve all mental energy. Utilize it for higher spiritual purposes, in divine contemplation, Brahma-Chintana and Brahma-Vichara. Conserve all thought-energy and utilize it for meditation and helpful service to humanity.

Drive away from your mind all unnecessary, useless and obnoxious thoughts. Useless thoughts impede your spiritual growth; obnoxious thoughts are stumbling blocks to spiritual advancement.

You are away from God when you entertain useless thoughts. Substitute thoughts of God. Entertain only thoughts that are helpful and useful.

Useful thoughts are the stepping-stones to spiritual growth and progress. Do not allow the mind to run into the old grooves and have its own ways and habits. Be on the careful watch.

Help the World by Good Thoughts

Like attracts like. If you entertain an evil thought, that thought attracts all sorts of evil thoughts from other people. You pass on those thoughts to others also.

Thought moves. Thought is a living dynamic force. Thought is a thing. If you allow your mind to dwell on a sublime thought this thought will attract good thoughts from others.

You pass on that good thought to others. You pollute the world with your bad thoughts.

Thought Power and the Conditions of a New Civilization

Thought makes man. Man makes civilization. There is a powerful thought-force behind every great event in life and in the history of the world.

Behind all discoveries and inventions, behind all religions and philosophies, behind all life-saving or life-destroying devices is thought.

Thought is expressed in words and executed in deeds. Word is the handmaid of thought, and deed is the end-result. Hence, the saying, "As you think, so you become."

How to build a new civilization?

By generating a new thought-force.

How to build a civilization that will ensure the peace of mankind, the prosperity of society, the salvation of the individual?

By generating a thought-force that will invariably result in man enjoying peace of mind, that will instill in his heart the divine virtues of compassion, of service to his fellow-men, love of God, and of an intense desire to realize Him.

If but a fraction of the wealth and the time spent on wasteful pursuits and destructive activities is devoted to the creation of a GOOD THOUGHT, there will be a new civilization right now.

Atomic and hydrogen bombs, I.C.B.M. and a host of other inventions drive mankind inevitably to destruction.

They waste your wealth; they destroy your neighbours; they pollute the atmosphere of the whole world, and generate fear, hatred, and suspicion in your heart; the mind is unbalanced and the body is subjected to diseases. Stop this trend.

Promote research in spirituality, in religion, in all the good things of life. Support the philosophers and saints—the real benefactors of mankind. Encourage them in their study of religion, researches in ancient spiritual literature, and the projection of a great thought-force for the good.

Ban all literature that pollutes the thoughts of the young. Flood the young brain with healthy thoughts, ideas and ideals.

The man who commits murder, the man who steals your purse, the man who cheats you—law punishes him. But this crime is insignificant when compared to the crime committed by the wicked intellectual who instills a wicked idea into the mind of youth.

He is the author of many murders that take place on earth; he steals your greatest wealth, viz., wisdom; he cheats you by presenting you with poison in the name of sweet elixir. The law of the new civilization will deal very severely with such Asuric beings.

The new civilization will give every encouragement to those who wish to study philosophy, religion and spiritual thought. It will make their study compulsory in schools and colleges. It will award scholarships to students of philosophy. It will confer prizes and titles on those who conduct researches in religion and philosophy. The deepest urge in man—the spiritual urge—will be given the fullest scope to realize its goal.

The fruits of the New Civilization are well worth all that everybody can do towards building it up. In the New Civilization man will want to lead a righteous life, he will be eager to serve his fellow-beings and share with them what he has; he will love all, realizing that his own Self dwells in all; he will be devoted to the welfare of all beings.

What an ideal society it will be, where people share with others all that they possess, and will serve everybody! Where will be the need for taxes and duties in such a society in which everyone will voluntarily work for all? Where is the need for police and the army when people are devoted to virtue?

This then is the ideal. Towards this end, let everyone strive to generate a Thought-force.

May God bless you all!